A Brief History of Nirze Village of Gesaria

Senekerim Khederian

Originally Armenian edition printed in 1918

Translated, edited, annotated and introduction
by Gerard J. Libaridian

Gomidas Institute
London

Support for *A Brief History of Nirze Village of Gesaria*
was provided by the generous support of the
M. Victoria Karagozian Kazan and
Henry S. Khanzadian Kazan Endowment of the
Armenian Studies Program at California State University, Fresno.

Gerard J. Libaridian is a retired historian and diplomat currently residing in Cambridge, Mass., USA, and working on a number of projects on modern and contemporary Armenian issues.

Original in Armenian:
Համառօտ պատմութիւն Կեսարիոյ Նիրզէ գիւղի
[A Brief History of Nirze Village of Gesaria]

English edition translated, edited, annotated and introduced by Gerard J. Libaridian with assistant editor Aram Sarkisian.

Prepared for publication by Nora Vosbigian.

Published by Gomidas Institute.

ISBN 978-1-909382-66-4

© 2021 by Gomidas Institute.

For comments and more information please contact:
Gomidas Institute
42 Blythe Rd
London W14 0HA
Email: *info@gomidas.org*
Web: *www.gomidas.org*

TABLE OF CONTENTS

Notes	v
Editor/Translator's Introduction	vii
Preface	1
Gesaria	
Brief information	5

Chapter I

Nirze Village and our forefathers	11
Weddings in Nirze	12
The organizations of Nirze	14
1909	14
The earthquake	16
The waters of Nirze	16
Mount Erciyes	16
The school of Nirze	17
The Meadow of Nirze (Nirze Chayere)	18
Soorp Krikor Monastery	18
Gat-Aghpyur [The Milk Fountain]	19
The Hole Stone [Dzag Kare]	21
Nirze's position	21
The Monday of Great Lent	22
The 1896 event in Nirze	23
About the priest, once again	24

Chapter II

The extended Khederian family	27
My father's life and death	27
My mother's life and death	32
My paternal aunts	37
My sister	38
My paternal uncles and their lives	41
[About me] From my birth to the present day	43
To America	46
My brothers	51

A Brief History of Nirze Village of Gesaria

Vahan	53
My paternal cousins	53
Garabed S. Khederian	54
Baruyr and Sarkis [my younger brothers]	54
My maternal uncle and his sons	57
Haji Boghos Haji Sarkissian	57
Hovhannes Kuyumjian	60
Asdur Kuyumjian	63
"News from Nirze"	64

Chapter III

Nirzetis in America	64
The lifestyle of Nirzetsis of America and our "union"	68
General list of Nirzetis by city	69
Those who returned to the Homeland	73
The life of Nirzetsis in America	75
Armenag Pavlian	77
Nirzetsis who died in America	77
Hayg Abajian	78
Krikor Balian	78
Stepan Alyanakian	78
Hapet Kehyayan	79
Nirzetsi volunteers	79
Diar [Sir] Vahan Kurkjian	80
Volunteers to the Caucasus front	85
On the path to duty	85
Last Minute	89

The [Armenian] Population of Nirze Village and Their Wealth (Before the 1914 War)	89

Notes

Translating and editing a work of this genre presents many challenges.

The following notes would help readers follow the narrative with a better understanding of the ways some issues have been resolved.

* In the case of individual or family names, to render the sound of the Armenian diphthong իւ, as u in lune in French, the German ü has been used as in für.

* The Western Armenian transliterated system has been used for the names of persons and places, except for a few historical names that have set forms, such as Tigran the Great for Մեծն Տիգրան, Grigor Lusavorich for Գրիգոր Լուսաւորիչ (Gregory the Illuminator), Soorp for սուրբ or holy.

* Bolis (Պոլիս) is the name used by Armenians for Bolis; it is short for the Armenian name of the city, Constantinople. Bolis has been kept in the translation.

* Words and explanations in brackets in the text have been inserted by the translator/editor for clarification. Items in parentheses are from the original text.

* The place of some segments has been changed in this edition without changing any of the contents, with the exception of a minor consolidation of the discussion of Vahan Kurkjian in two different places in order to avoid repetition.

* A two-page section at the end of the original text titled "Philosophical thoughts" was not included in this edition since these were personal observations that did not contribute to the text in any way.

* The Table of Contents in this edition corrects a few errors found in the original and reflects the arrangement of segments in this book.

* The "tsi" (ցի) suffix in Armenian, added to a place name, means a person born in or from that place. A Nirzetsi, for example, is a person who was born or lived in Nirze.

* We have reproduced all photographs from the original Armenian work and supplemented them with additional photographs and a map.

The translator/editor is thankful to Mr. Harry Parsekian of Watertown, Massachusetts, for initiating this project and otherwise facilitating its completion and publication.

Many thanks also to Mr. Sinan Mordağ of Turkey for his assistance in filling some of the gaps in Khederian's work.

The translator/editor is most grateful, finally, to Dr. Aram Sarkisian for his invaluable editorial assistance.

Editor/Translator's Introduction

"A Brief History of Nirze Village of Gesaria" is one in a large genre of the Armenian written word known as "compatriotic" narratives. For the most part, these works were undertaken after the Genocide initiated in 1915 by the Ottoman Turkish government, which depopulated most of the Ottoman Empire of its Armenian population, including historical Western Armenia. By various accounts there are anywhere from 200 to 350 such volumes, large and small, depending on the varying criteria of those who have catalogued such works. The purpose of these volumes was to record for posterity the social and political lives of Armenians in villages, cities, and entire regions where their people once lived. For survivors, to immortalize lives and environments that were lost to the Genocide became an irresistible mission. Their books were a means to memorialize their birthplaces, but more importantly, a form of respect for the dead, the insistence that their memories were not forgotten.

Some of the authors of these "compatriotic history" volumes were either professional or semi-professional researchers and writers. Many treated the subject systematically, and included not only a history and geography of the location in question, but also descriptions of customs, descriptions of institutions, dictionaries for the dialects, songs, sayings, lists of survivors settled in different countries, histories of the compatriotic union in question, and biographies of prominent and successful compatriots in the Diaspora.

Others, like Senekerim Khederian, were one-time authors with varying degrees of competence. Khederian was a literate man, but not a professional writer. Though not particularly a voluminous book, the mere existence of his work served to distinguish Nirze from many other villages of the same size and general significance. So many others did not have their own Senekerim Khederian, an author who honored his birthplace with a monument of memories and words.

We should note that this is the first known work of its kind, works known as the "compatriotic books." Some such works written before the First World War belong in the ethnographic category and do not reflect the deep sense of loss and pain that compatriotic books project.

Khederian's booklet was written in 1917 and published in 1918, as the massacres and deportations were winding down. Thus, Khederian's pain is accompanied by a sense of hope that there would be a return, despite the losses. Compatriotic books were written years and decades after the Genocide, when realization had set in that there would be no return to or revival of the historic Western Armenian homeland. As such it can be considered a unique and pioneering work.

The author

Senekerim Khederian was born in 1890 to a large family in the village of Nirze, northeast of the major city of Gesaria (Kayseri in Turkish). Senekerim was his family's second son. He attended the village school, and had the equivalent of a junior high school education, though one which included the teaching of foreign languages and Ottoman law. He worked in his father's grocery store for a time, then migrated to America at age nineteen to join his eldest brother, Garabed, in Watertown, Massachusetts. His younger brother, Vahan, followed suit. During the First World War, Vahan volunteered for the Armenian Legion of the French Army and served as an officer. The younger siblings were never heard from during, nor after the massacres and deportations. They were presumed killed, or in the case of young women like their sister, more than likely abducted by Turks.

Senekerim was married to Loutfyah (Mary) and had two daughters. He lived in Watertown on Lloyd Road. He became a naturalized citizen in 1929. He owned a restaurant across the street from the "club," associated with the Tashnagtsutiun (ARF) party, where Armenian men gathered to drink coffee, play backgammon and cards, exchange news about their village and Armenia, argue about politics, and gossip. (The club continues to function today as the Armenian-American Social Club, 76 Bigelow Avenue, Watertown.) Senekerim Khederian died in 1958.

On the history of the book

Oral tradition has it that Nirzetsis in the United States, particularly those in Watertown, asked Senekerim Khederian to write the history of the village as a tribute to their birthplace and lost families. The urgency to have a history of their village was in response to two contradictory reflexes: the sense that the village as they knew it, along with their families and homes, was lost, and their hope against hope they would be able to return and reconstruct their village. They paid Khederian for that assignment. Many were unhappy with the result, however, since they thought the author had spent too many pages on his own family.

Even so, the book was published in 1918 (the preface was completed in September 1917). Although no place of publication is indicated anywhere in the book, one can presume the 146-page, small format volume (5¼ x 7⅕ inches), was printed in the Boston area. Copies were sold for one dollar. A notice at the beginning and at the end of the book indicated that "All proceeds from the sale of the book will be used for the reconstruction of Nirze Village of Gesaria." Another notice, printed at the end of the book, assured buyers that "The accounting related to the book will be supervised by the Executive Committee of the Educational Association of Nirze Village of Gesaria."

Khederian's text became a source for the section on Nirze in Arshag Alboyajian's monumental, two-volume *Badmoutiun Hay* Gesario [History of Armenian Gesaria], (Cairo, 1937, Volume 1, pages 796-801).

The original Armenian version was reproduced in Armenia sometime after independence, though without identifying its publisher, date, place, or any other information.

In 2015 Harry Parsekian, a lifelong resident of Watertown, Massachusetts, edited a small volume, Armenians of Nirze, Turkey: Roots of an Armenian-American. In addition to providing information on the village of Nirze, the birthplace of his parents, Parsekian offers the story of three Nirzetsis who recorded their memoirs as survivors of the Genocide; he also updates the story of Nirzetis in America and offers his thoughts upon visiting Nirze and connecting with its current residents. In preparing his work, Parsekian relies heavily on Senekerim Khederian's volume. Harry Parsekian's work is a necessary companion to this one. Parsekian also inspired the undertaking and completion of this, the publication in English of Khederian's work.

Sinan Mordağ, a Turkish actor and cultural activist of Nirze, has just completed a major study of Nirze Village in Turkish, one that will inlcude Khederian's work in translation. Mordağ's work will present a detailed account of the centuries-old history of the village including the full story of its inhabitants from the earliest times. Khederian relates the story of its

Armenian population only. Mordağ's volume has been scheduled for publication during the current year.

Style and form

Khederian's book has three parts. The first is about the village, the second concerns the Khederian clan, and the third focuses on Nirzetsis in America. In writing this book, the author has done his best to do justice to his village, as did others who were not professional writers or researchers. As detailed in the notes, in this edition I have rearranged the position of some segments to make it easier for the reader to follow his text, without changing any of the contents or context.

I should also note that when translating the volume, I rendered some of the Armenian and Turkish terms and idioms in the original language in order to offer the reader a flavor of the narrative and style, while providing the English equivalent next to that word in brackets.

In relating his stories, the author has often used the past and present tenses interchangeably, depending on his sense, it appears, as to what is lost and what is still there. Reflecting that sense of the author, the translation has preserved the author's usage of the two tenses.

Significance of the book for researchers

It is possible for readers to find Khederian's narrative somewhat self-absorbed, since his story is as much about his family and himself as about Nirze. Yet the story of the family emerges as a microcosm of the Armenian world as it evolved, changed, spread, suffered and sang in the years preceding, during, and following the war that so decimated its people and communities.

In addition to offering precious details of institutional life, the author describes his family and clan using details that inject a human dimension into the lives of villagers, even if a bit too intimately at times. In his approach, Khederian displays both respect for traditions and customs but also criticism of old prejudices and tales. Thus, the volume has significance for researchers in a number of areas: ethnography, sociology, political science, history, psychology and social psychology. Among others, these are themes that can be explored through this book:

Editor/Translator's Introduction

* Clan and family social relations, the joys and sorrows of a normal life, deaths and marriages, conflicting interests and attitudes behind the veil of idyllic sounding memories
* The decisive role of women in village and family life, including as income earners and pillars of stability and continuity
* The functions of national institutions like the Armenian Apostolic Church, and political parties as they operate at the local level
* The significance of class in determining relations and major decisions in the village
* The relationship between Ottoman government policy, Armenian institutions, and village life
* The simultaneous introduction of processes of modernization and needs for self-defense, and the village's responses to such changes
* The migration of young men to America as itinerant workers, and the dire consequences of that phenomenon for demographic realities in the homeland
* The impact of the news of massacres and deportations in the homeland on young men in America. This included the debilitating effect of not knowing the fate of family members left behind, the pain of having survived and, perhaps aside from those who joined volunteer regiments, common feelings of incapacity to help
* The formation of the Armenian Diaspora prior to the Genocide, and the ensuing influx of survivors from the historic homeland
* The transformation of a village community in the homeland into a compatriotic union in the Diaspora
* A most valuable list of Nirzetsis in America before the war, what their numbers mean relative to the families they left behind, a possible source for studies of acculturation and assimilation
* An equally valuable list of Armenian households of Nirze, the number of members in each household, and the financial worth of each family.

The volume has gaps in many areas. These include any information on non-Armenian residents of the village, the total picture of its inhabitants, relations between the various ethnic/religious groups, and governance of the village.

In early nineteenth century, according to one source, Nirze was a village of "three nations," Armenians, Turks, and Greeks totaling 300 households. Khederian lists 150/151 Armenian households extant immediately before the First World War. One source refers to a total number of 160 households at the end of the nineteenth century, equally divided between Armenian and Turkish families. Information from other sources indicates that there might have been as many as 186 Armenian households. It is also clear from other sources, that there may have been as many Turkish households as Armenian ones. According to Sinan Mordağ, Turkish Nirzetis had a mosque and a school. And yet Turkish residents are mentioned only once in the book: Khederian relates that Turkish villagers saved the village during the 1896 massacres; Turkish neighbors stood in the way of the mob intent on murdering Armenians and looting their belongings; confronting the attackers with their weapons, they threatened to shoot if attackers moved toward the Armenian quarters.

In terms of governance, Mordağ also indicates that the village had a Turkish chief, while an Armenian hokapartsutiun (council) managed Armenian community affairs, a body that is not mentioned by Khederian. The village had regular visits, according to Mordağ, by a müdür, (inspector) from the Ottoman government müdürlük (inspectorate), to ensure that all was in order. A judge and gendarmes [armed police], from Gesaria or Efkere would also visit Nirze in case of need.

In spite of its shortcomings, this small volume brings to life a village and one of its families at a time of cataclysmic change in the Ottoman Empire, as recorded by a native son who found safety and comfort in America. The immediacy with which Khederian writes manages to recreate a world threatened by economic and political change, a re-creation that acquires greater importance by the destruction of its Armenian component through war and genocide.

Gerard J. Libaridian
Cambridge, Mass.
March 2021

A Brief History of Nirze Village of Gesaria

Preface

The purpose of this book is to introduce Nirze Village and not to allow memories that are dear to us to be forgotten. In preparation for this book, I have appealed to all Nirzetsis without exception and asked for their biographies and photographs. Unfortunately, few responded to my requests.

Initially I did not have the intention to write such a book. But events compelled me to undertaking this difficult task.

My compatriots should be forgiving if some dates and ages are off by a year. As I said, it is quite difficult to remember the date and time of events.

I was content to read in detail approximately 400 letters. I have been in America for seven years and various personalities have written to me in detail concerning the events that occurred during those years.

My book contains many biographical notes; it is doubtless that they will include many errors. For these too I ask for the forgiveness of my compatriots.

The book represents 100 years of the history of Nirze Village. I have benefited from the stories of our grandfathers and grandmothers.

We left back in the homeland our parents, brothers and sisters, relatives and friends; we miss them. We want to converse with them through letters and refresh our nostalgia-stricken hearts. But, alas, we were deprived even of that possibility.

I was compelled to write to Nirzetsis living in different corners of America to gather information and to summarize the story of the village in this book to the best of my ability.

The ceasing of letters from our dear ones and the catastrophe that befell us made it necessary that I publish this book. Throughout its existence humankind has always sought happiness as its guiding light, and wanted to achieve that happiness in freedom. The Armenian people, too, being part of humankind, strove for liberty. But it was necessary to struggle to achieve that liberty. Unfortunately, we were surrounded by a savage tribe, devoid of elementary civilization, of common consciousness, devoid also of human ideas, incapable of judging things by their value. That tribe had adopted only one principle: to massacre and to destroy. And that is why the Armenian people suffered the most in this world-shaking war, and why their existence is threatened. Many towns and villages are in ruins today. This includes Nirze Village.

Before I sent the manuscript of this book to press, I received a letter from Gesaria.[1] The poor author wrote: "I am still alive as a consequence of my being an ironsmith... Though the wolf ate all the sheep, don't be concerned." This short, but effective sentence contains much meaning. It makes us think that the Nirzetsis were all massacred or deported. Having with us the descriptions of Nirze's water, air, mountains, and ravines as relics and memories transmitted to our next generation, then, is worth the effort.

>Senekerim
>September 20, 1917
>Watertown

---

1. Gesaria is the Armenian name of the main city in central Turkey, known previously as Caesaria and currently as Kayseri. It was and still is a major commercial and industrial hub served by a large number of satellite village, Nirze being one of them.

Senekerim Khederian, the author (from the original Armenian edition, most probably Boston, date and photographer unknown).

A Brief History of Nirze Village of Gesaria

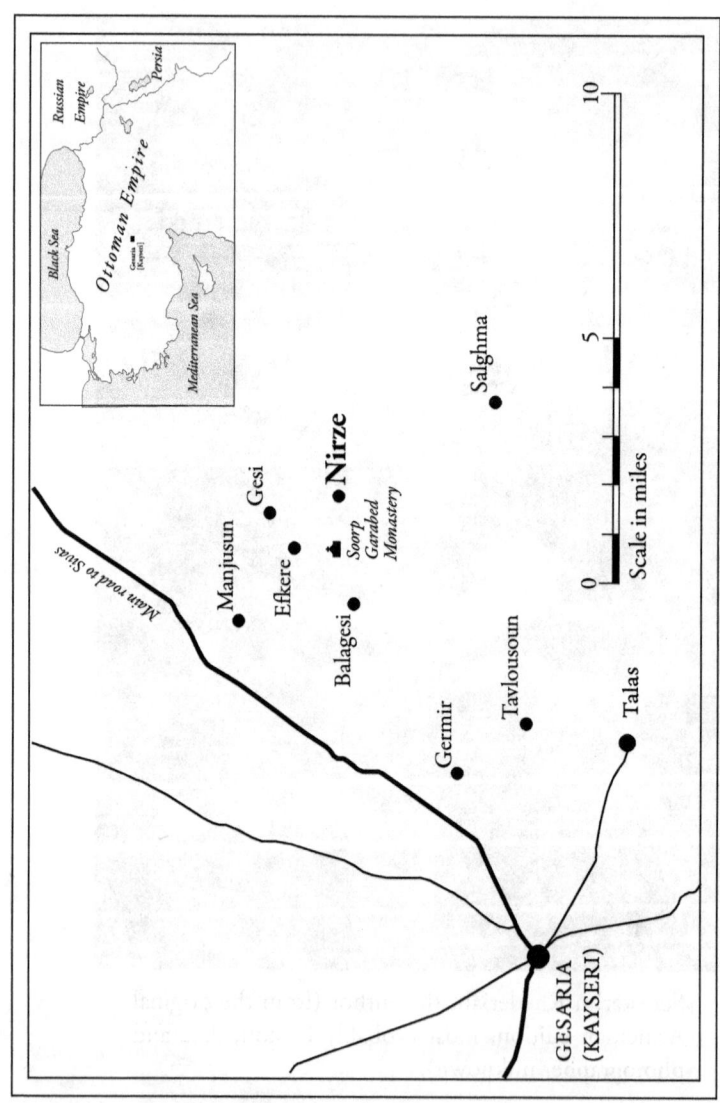

Map of Gesaria [Kayseri]-Nirze [Güzelköy].

Gesaria

Brief Information

According to the traditional history of Armenians,[2] the domination of the Haygazun dynasty started during the time of King Aram, son of Harma, and expanded in many directions of the land.

There are many mythical stories around Aram. Among the Haygazun Kings, Aram is known as the builder of more public projects than any other. He was a king who established and kept contact with Armenians spread all over the country. Aram Nahabed [patriarch] defeated many kings and conquered many lands. His most important victory was over the prince of Cappadocia, and his best-known battle was against Bayabis Kaghia. Aram attacked Cappadocia with an army of 60,000 and chased Bayabis Kaghia all the way to the shores of the Mediterranean. With these victories Aram expanded the western borders of Armenia. Aram named the areas he conquered in the following manner: First Hayk, Second Hayk, Third Hayk, Fourth Hayk; at the end these lands were those collectively called Small Hayk (Armenia Minor). Aram appointed the general named Mshag, known as a builder himself, to govern these territories (1300 BCE) and instructed that the use of the Armenian language be obligatory for all inhabitants, so that they all would be Armenianized. Mshag built a city in his own name, and Greeks, unable to pronounce the name, called it Mazhak. That is the city, which was taken from the Greeks by Julius Caesar, reconstructed, and renamed Gesaria (Caesaria).

The Armenian Empire was established during the time of Tigran [Tigranes] the Great (84 BCE). It was Tigran the Great who started reconquering lands lost by his predecessors. Tigran the Great's armies reached all the way to Egypt, conquered the cities of Palestine, and made Jews his subjects. The Armenian flag flew over Damascus, Tyre, and other Phoenician cities. It was during Tigran's reign that Jews settled in Armenia. Tigran ruled over the Assyrians, who had a prosperous life under him. Intent on world domination, Tigran marched toward Cilicia to defeat

---

2. It is important to note that the author's rendering of Armenian history in the next few pages is indeed "traditional," but also based on popularized stories and should not be taken literally. For a more reliable narrative, please refer to general survey histories of the Armenian people by scholars such as Richard, G. Hovhannisian.

the last remnants of the Seleucid rulers. He destroyed many Cilician cities and moved their populations to Armenia. It was then that Tigran conquered Cappadocia, as well as Mazhak or Gesaria and other cities for the third time. He forcibly moved the Greek population, numbering 300,000, to Tigranagerd [literally "built by Tigran"], the new capital city of the King of Kings (77 BCE).

During the Arshaguni [Arsacid] era, King Khosrov engaged in war with Persia's King Shapur I. At that time Armenians were allied with the Caesar of Rome, Philip. The latter was forced to sign a shameful treaty with Shapur I and denounced Khosrov to Shapur. Khosrov was compelled to continue the war on his own. Unable to defeat the Armenians in battle, Shapur I used treachery. One of the princes of the Surenian *dohm* [the extended princely family], Anag Bahlavuni (Grigor Lusavorich's father), took upon himself to put the treachery into effect. Pretending that he was running away from the Persian king, he came to Armenia with his whole family. Being a relative of Khosrov, Anag gained his confidence and was entrusted with high positions and one day assassinated the Armenian king. Before he died, Khosrov gave the name of the assassin. The Armenian *nakharars* [princes] took revenge for their king's murder by throwing Anag Bartev and his associates from the bridge, and by killing his descendants. That was the day when the Persian king Shapur I rid himself from a dangerous foe. The roads to Armenia were open; he entered Armenia and drove out the Roman soldiers. The nakharars started to flee. Ardavazt Mantaguni took Khosrov's son Drtad [Tiridates] and fled to Rome, and prince Dajad took one of Ardavazt's sisters to Gesaria and married her. Toward the end of the Arsacid period, the Persian King Vram recognized the suzerainty of Rome and signed a peace treaty regarding Armenia.

Emperor Diocletian recognized Drtad as king of Armenia and sent him back to Armenia with a large army. A number of nakharars welcomed the king in Gesaria and, surrounded by them, Drtad entered Armenia as a liberator.

Drtad had an enlightened mind and the light of Christianity was brought to him by Grigor Lusavorich [Gregory the Illuminator],[3] who was

---

3. Grigor is known as the Lusavorich or Illuminator, since he is reported to be responsible for convincing King Drtad of Armenia to convert to Christianity and make it the state religion, sometime around 301 CE.

the son of Anag the Parthian, who killed Drtad's father. When Anag's family was exterminated in the hands of vengeful Armenian nakharars, Grigor was the only one who was saved from Anag's family. Grigor was taken to Gesaria by his savior. In Gesaria, Grigor grew up receiving a Christian and Hellenistic education. Grigor joined Drtad when Drtad returned to Armenia. There are many mythical stories that describe what occurred between Drtad and Grigor at that time. Following these events, Grigor Lusavorich, accompanied by sixteen notable nakharars, ceremoniously traveled to Gesaria and was consecrated chief bishop or catholicos of the Armenians by the Greek metropolitan Ghevont [Leontius] and other bishops (302 CE).

The church where Grigor Lusavorich was consecrated catholicos[4] was converted to a mosque during the reign of Sultan Fatih. That mosque is now called Huat Mosque and is the prominent one in Gesaria.

Gesaria has three churches. Soorp [Saint] Sarkis, Soorp Astvadzadzin and Soorp Grigor. There are schools next to the churches. Gesaria had a very well-organized education system; the courses taught in these schools were at a higher level than in any of the missionary schools. Also, close to Gesaria was Soorp Garabed Monastery, where between one hundred and two hundred youngsters studied. Any graduate from Soorp Garabed Monastery was looked upon with respect by schools and readily given teaching positions.

Part of the city of Gesaria is surrounded by an ancient wall. The whole city is adorned with beautiful buildings, gardens, and army barracks. Gesaria was a trade center between East and West in the olden days, though not so much currently, but it still continues its famed and envious trade skills. Currently Gesaria's trade is the most profitable in Asia Minor. The people of Gesaria are wonderfully clever and active. Armenians, well known for their trade skills, owe most of their fame to Gesaratsis. The best-known merchants in Europe and elsewhere, and especially in Bolis[5] (Istanbul, Constantinople), are Gesaratsis. The market of Gesaria is built in an artful manner the like of which cannot be found in any other country. As the city has grown, the wall, with its smaller arc, has been engulfed by it. And the wall has increasingly become weaker and shakier

---

4. Catholicos is the title of the head of the Armenian Apostolic Church.
5. Bolis is the name Armenians use for Istanbul, Constantinople.

since the Turkish domination. The areas surrounded by the wall are inhabited by Turkish families. It is said that women in Turkish harems do not know what an Armenian is: Is the Armenian a human being or an animal? It is absolutely forbidden for them to leave their houses.

The Hnchagian Party[6] has done considerable work in Gesaria, no one can deny it. However, the party was left in disarray after the split in the party.[7] Therefore, with a few exceptions, its branches were dissolved in Gesaria. They did exist in spots in the city and in some villages but they no longer represented the required strength. The Armenian Revolutionary Federation [ARF],[8] which was already present in Gesaria, expanded and became strong after the Constitution.[9] The Tashnags published a weekly, *Hayeg*, that was very useful, especially for Gesaratsis living in the US, who were kept abreast of developments in Gesaria through that publication. But *Hayeg* ceased publication on the first day of the war [1914]. Gesaria boasted of the ARF Krisdapor[10] library, an impressive building in the most famous part of the city. The party grew and spread day by day in the city, as well as in the villages. Party affairs were led by Vahan Effendi[11] Kurkjian of Nirze (Director General of Gesaria schools) and Doctor Khachig Doevletian. Turkish barbarity put an end to that dynamic mission.

The city founded by Aram has a history of 3000 years, but today it lies in ruins. The monumental trade is destroyed, and the Armenian

---

6. The Social Democratic Hnchagian Party, also known as Hnchags or Hnchagians, the first Armenian revolutionary party devoted to the liberation of Western Armenia, founded in 1887/1888.
7. The Hnchagian party split after the 1894-1896 massacres of Armenians in the Ottoman Empire. The split was between hardline socialists and those who thought the struggle against Ottoman oppression should be based more on the national dimension.
8. Hay Heghapokhagan Tashnagtsutiun is the second Armenian revolutionary party aimed at the liberation of Armenians from Ottoman rule. Established in 1890, it is also known as Tashnagtsutiun, or Tashnags.
9. This is a reference to the "National Constitution" of the Armenians in the Ottoman Empire, approved in 1863. The document regulated and democratized the areas where Armenians had a degree extraterritorial self-governance in civil affairs within the structure of the Armenian Apostolic Church.
10. Krisdapor Mikayelian is one of the three founders of the ARF.
11. Effendi is a Turkish honorific.

Site of Soorp Garabed Monastery postcard before 1915.

Part of Soorp Krikor Monastery (2020, photographer unknown. Courtesy of Sinan Mordağ).

population is exterminated. But this is not the first time Gesaria has endured such storms. Those who know history are aware that Gesaria was an apple of discord between Greeks and Armenians, and that it was very vulnerable. But it has remained solid like an oak tree and no storm can obliterate it.

It is us Gesaratsis who will go to revive it again, and to reestablish a flourishing trade. I am hopeful that our Gesaratsi compatriots will return to the land, which has so much history behind it and is adored by every Gesaratsi.

Chapter 1

Nirze Village and our forefathers

Judging from the ruins of ancient structures, Nirze Village is a few thousand years old. Our forefathers relate that the village was established largely by refugees from Dersiyah, Geomurgen and Gassieh.

As recently as 1852, ten refugee families came from Tomarza. According to Armenian tradition, the village became divided between the old and new residents, who fought each other. Finally, the old ones were able to drive the refugees from Tomarza out of the village. The latter, it is said, roamed from Turkish village to Turkish village for four or five years.[12]

Through the mediation of the then-prelate, Bishop Hagop, the feuding ended and the refugees returned to Nirze. It is for that reason that some of the old villagers beat up Bishop Hagop quite badly in Soorp Garabed Monastery. Finally, there was reconciliation and the village had a peaceful life for thirty to forty years. At that time the village had fifty to sixty households.

The village had a series of parish priests, among them was the late Father Stepan. Being extremely conservative, he had achieved nothing positive for the village. Because of his partisanship, village life had become absolutely chaotic. But the villagers had not remained indifferent. They campaigned passionately against the priest. They removed him from the altar a few times during liturgy, and on occasion, fights had broken out in the church[13] about the priest, or because of him. Father Stepan was so scared of Sultan Hamid that when singing *Der Voghormia* ["Lord Have Mercy"] he would replace the words "give freedom to our nation" with "give love and unity to our nation." There also occurred some ugly incidents during his time as spiritual pastor that I will not describe in this book. He passed away around 1905. After his death the villagers presented the names of five or six candidates. The result was disputes among the

---

12. The reason for the conflict could have been the fact that Tomarzatsis were Armenian speaking while Nirzetis were, for the most part, Turkish speaking.
13. The author does not mention the name of the church, Soorp (St.) Toros.

Soorp Toros Church, (2020, photographer unknown.
Courtesy of Sinan Mordağ).

candidates, who neutralized each other. At the end no candidate was chosen. The villagers were compelled to bring in outsiders. One of those was Father Karekin, who was a liberal, revolutionary, brave, and strong priest, the likes of whom can rarely be found. During the Adana massacres[14] he not only tried to organize the village but also he himself learned how to make explosives. He made many dozens and sold them to Armenians in Nirze and other villages. But unfortunately, someone informed the government about him and he was jailed. But he was soon released because of his clever tongue.

Weddings in Nirze

Weddings in Nirze involve an odd custom. Without getting into detail, let me say only that it required that the side of the bride-to-be be robbed blind, to the extent that anyone whose daughter was getting married would spend as much as the groom's side. On the surface, the only thing that might leave a positive impression is that on Sunday, when the wedding

---

14. Refers to massacres of Armenians in towns and villages in and around Cilicia organized by Turkish conservatives in reaction to the reinstatement of the Ottoman Constitution in 1908, which recognized the equality of all subjects, regardless of religion. Close to 30,000 Armenians were massacred on that occasion throughout Cilicia; the event is also known as the Adana massacres.

Chapter 1

ceremony in the church ends, they put on a white church *shabig* [altar server's vestment] on the groom and a *sparmachet*[15] candle in his hand, then they have him stand next to the priest, and all guests kiss the crown of the new groom, without exception.[16]

Thousands have believed, along with me, that the newlywed couple feel that they were born only on that day. Oh, would every young man enjoy that glory and pleasures which in human life are deemed worthy of a kingdom.

Following that ceremony, everyone waits for the arrival of the groom in the churchyard. The groom then leaves the church with the "*Hrashapar*" [The hymn "Wonderous Glory"], the bride next to him, surrounded by a number of young Armenian girls and women. According to this custom, called "*enge*," the procession is accompanied by the priest, led by the lesser clergy with church bells in hand [a censer?], who are singing wonderful church songs.[17] The people follow the groom. Enthusiasm dominates the hearts of the guests. The bride, as I indicated, surrounded by young ladies and women, follows the people by slow steps. I wonder what young man does not think about enjoying the same fortune, to see relatives and friends prepare anise drink or wine to honor the traveling guests?

It has been a custom in the village to sacrifice a rooster at the feet of the bride and groom, whether the newlyweds are rich or poor. These are customs of consolation. There are also disgraceful, negative phenomena, though I will refrain from describing them.

---

15. It has not been possible to identify the word *sparmachet*. Most likely it refers to an imported brand of candle, possibly used for special occasions.
16. This tradition echoes a custom after the ordination of a priest, when the newly-ordained stands at the chancel and his anointed hands are venerated in a similar way. The custom of singing of Hrashapar and of a procession is borrowed from other aspects of church ritual, all of which involve the veneration or exaltation of a priest or bishop.
17. What he may be describing here is a բշնգ, *kshots*. A kshots is a long rod with a ceremonial fan and bells on top. Deacons would certainly carry that in a procession. What he says here makes sense, as the order of a procession would usually be deacons and lesser clergy followed by the priest, and they would probably carry a kshots.

The organizations of Nirze

It is true that the Hnchagian Party was a presence in Nirze. But that lasted only a few months before it thinned out and subsequently disappeared, wholly due to the terror created by Sultan Abdul Hamid.

The village remained without an organization until 1908. Soon after the reinstatement of the Constitution, some young men organized a union with the purpose of locally securing weapons and explosives. The name of the organization was "Union of Armenian Progressive Youth." They started recruiting members, organizing weekly meetings and lectures. They ended up with between thirty and forty members and earned considerable interest from the villagers. And then, hardly a month had passed when there appeared a second union, which was named … .[18] Thus started the battle of spoken and written words and flyers. Their activities crossed each other; there were often fights during meetings, when they threw chairs at one another. In short, unspeakable disgraces.

I have heard from a reliable source that at that time, Doctor Kh. Deovletian intervened through his representatives but was unable to settle the fighting. After a few months they came to an understanding and they came together. But many of the members had resigned, having been turned off by the fighting. They also publicly urged others "not to become members," [because] "the money you give is used by them to get together in the evenings to eat pears and apples under the guise of being in meetings." Even though they merged, unfortunately these unions have not accomplished anything positive; the few pounds of explosives they had was left to a few individuals, without anyone taking responsibility for them.

1909

The wretched Nirzetsis were so afraid of the horrors of Sultan Abdul Hamid[19] that they severely scolded anyone who spoke of organizations or

---

18. The author does not provide the name of the second organization and provides no reason for that omission. He may have simply forgotten it.

19. The Ottoman Sultan Abdul Hamid II (reigned from 1876 to 1909) is known as the Red Sultan for his incitement of the 1894-1896 massacres of Armenians throughout Ottoman Turkey and for his oppressive, tyrannical rule. The Young Turk Revolution of 1908 stripped him of his authority, and he was dethroned in 1909.

Chapter 1

political parties. Therefore, the new generation that came to age was a perfectly conservative youth.

Over the years Armenians in our sister villages all organized themselves under the flag of the Armenian Revolutionary Federation, except in our village where not a voice was heard in that respect. Dr. Deovletian [visited Nirze] and made appeals a few times but returned without hope of success. Yet that changed.

Then came the massacre of Adana, and our villagers realized they were not at all prepared. They sensed that they would be slaughtered like sheep if they could not put up any resistance. In view of that, they hastened to convene a village-wide meeting. In addition to the prominent personalities of the village, the meeting was attended by those who were expert weapons users and old revolutionaries, among them my well-known uncle, Mr. Boghos Haji Sarkissian. The only item on the agenda of the meeting was what should we do in case of a Turkish assault. The lengthy discussion did not lead to a clear decision. The argument rested on the need for the wealthy to provide funds to buy weapons. Yet the wealthy, constituting the majority of those present, objected to that proposal. The solution proposed by the experienced Haji Boghos was also rejected, vehemently. He proposed that instead of going to the rich or the poor, the village might resort to another solution. When the enemy arrives tomorrow, argued Haji Boghos, he will not differentiate between rich and poor, he will not spare school or church. That being the case, the village church has many gold crosses and various vessels. Let us sell a few of them, the Church will not miss anything, and we will have achieved our purpose. But then they started screaming from right and left, "Dear God, to sell the cross? That is such faithlessness!" At the end they could not come to an agreement and the project was aborted. The meeting adjourned without having achieved anything.

Then there was an appeal that each household purchase self-defense weapons to the best of their financial ability. Thus a few young and old men began standing guard with old *chakhmakhli* [flintlock guns] and Martin rifles. Fortunately no incidents occurred, otherwise we would have been slaughtered like sheep.

The earthquake

Our forefathers would recall that in 1846, an earthquake struck, whose aftershocks shook the houses for three or four days. The villagers had to go to the threshing field and live in tents for weeks. During that time a few people were killed and some houses were destroyed.

The waters of Nirze

Nirze village is situated in the northeast of Gesaria, within a three-hour distance from the city. It has been erected in a beautiful dale, and is surrounded by vineyards and gardens.

A stream, strong enough to power a mill, passes through the dale. That stream irrigates the orchards of three or four villages. The stream's waters are considered very beneficial; they have also caused some bloodshed. Fighting for that water is an everyday occurrence. The name of that stream was Gogo Salghma (Salghma Su [Water]), because the stream originated in the Turkish village of Salghma. The following villages benefit from that stream: Salghma, two hours each day; Nirze, on Fridays and Saturdays; Gassi, on Sundays, Mondays and Tuesdays; and Manjon, Wednesdays and Thursdays. This was the arrangement for the use of the stream. In the villages you needed to wait for your turn. All households in Nirze had their vineyard or garden.

As I mentioned, Nirze is in a beautiful spot in a dale. It has clean air and well-designed streets. All streets without exception go uphill. Gesaratsis came to Nirze for relief from the summer heat. All houses are made of stone, simple, beautifully metal-crafted stones. Stone masons usually made smooth columns and threshold pieces. Architecture was well advanced in cities and villages; even markets were built with well hewn stones.

Mount Erciyes

Mount Erciyes is considered one of the highest in Asia. Its top is always covered with snow. Consequently, Gesaria, Talas, and many villages have clean and fresh air. Thousands of Gesaratsis spend their summers in areas close to Erjiesh. Turks publish a newspaper named after that mountain in Gesaria.

Chapter 1

The school of Nirze

Just as in other places, the school of Nirze was very backward until 1895. The Book of Psalms and the Book of Hours [*Zhamakirk*, a prayer book] were the only textbooks used. But after that date Nirzetsis adopted progressive policies. They built a school next to the church, which is at the highest point of Nirze and had the cleanest air. The school has a study area that can accommodate 150 to 200 students. It has a classroom, an inn, and a few other rooms. Next to these is also a dark and damp corner, which is called *sadanayadun* [home of Satan], or *jichig*.[20] Unruly and delinquent students were sent there as punishment. The school also has a nice garden, which teachers have the right to use. The old school was in ruins and the ground used as a playground for half an hour each day.[21]

Although not a new structure, the church is constructed beautifully and because of its position, it dominates the whole village. Recently a bell tower was added and its beautiful pealing could be heard a half hour away.

As I mentioned, with the reconstruction of the school there also was a renewal of the teachers. The Book of Psalms and Book of Hours were replaced by regular textbooks. The school budget jumped from fifteen or twenty gold liras to 100 by the 1910s. So, the school recently has had an enviable life. The Armenian, Turkish, English and French languages were taught there.

The number of teachers varied between two and three. Initially they were paid by the church. But more recently they were compensated from the tuition paid by students' families, each according to its ability.

There was a good custom in Nirze, which was to invite teachers in the homes of families on Sundays. There also was a bad habit, in that no teacher was kept for more than two years. The villagers always found something wrong with every teacher during those two years and, as a result, students hardly learned very much. Each teacher brought his own methods to the school and students were left behind. This is the main reason why village schools never improved.

---

20. It was not possible to determine the origins or meaning of this word.
21. The school was named "Torkomian."

The meadow of Nirze *(Nirze Chayere)*

Although Nirze had a number of meadows in different spots of the village, it also has a famous one, Nirze Chayere. The water that starts at Soorp Grigor reaches that meadow after running for only one minute. Nature has designed that meadow in such a way that it is surrounded by that beautiful running water. In the spring, colorful flowers start to bud and their aroma is sensed in all directions. After May, the students of the school begin their games in that meadow and almost all the young of the village gather there to play.

On Vartavar Day, which is the [feast] day of Soorp Garabed Monastery, pilgrims arrive from all parts of Pokr Hayk. The pilgrims spend their Sunday in the gardens of the monastery and in front of its gate. On the Monday, Merelotz, the Day of the Dead, all pilgrims, and Armenian and Turkish villagers from surrounding areas, gather at Nirze Chayere. They eat, drink, and dance there to the sound of many orchestras in an extremely joyous atmosphere.

Soorp Krikor Monastery

The monastery is built in a vale and is as old as can be. Looking at its structure, it may be a few thousand years old. Only the rampart of the old structure remains. It is not possible to erect a structure like it in our days. Its stones are of unhewn rocks. The rampart is about fifteen meters high. There is a dining hall within the walls that can accommodate forty to fifty people. Usually, pious women and girls assemble there on Saturday evenings in the summers to pray to the old God of the old monastery.

There is also a cave in the monastery; one can walk for ten minutes inside it. It is built with great ingenuity. In case of necessity there is a sufficient supply of water. Unfortunately, there is no date anywhere that could indicate how many thousands of years ago the cave was dug. People have sometimes found crosses and other religious vessels inside the cave. What is known as Nirze Su [Nirze Water] could run a mill and starts right inside the monastery. It is a bluish water, very cold in the summer, yet warm enough to emit steam in the winter. There are a number of tombstones by the door of the monastery. It is said that one of them is that of Gregory of Nyssa.[22] The land at the entrance of the monastery is sizable

---

22. Gregory of Nyssa (c. 335-395) is known as one of the Cappadocian Fathers, the founders of Christian theology.

enough to accommodate a house or a school. There is a beautiful garden inside the monastery which the parish priest of the village has the right to cultivate.

The old women of the village have a story they tell about one of the recent abbots of the monastery. As I mentioned, there was hot water at the entrance of the monastery, and the women and young girls of the village went there in the winter to do their washing. One day one of the women goes there with her four- or five-year-old son. Standing there the child either feels cold or gets bored and starts to cry. Apparently the abbot had been watching the scene from his second-floor window. He takes pity on the child and throws him an apple to stop the crying. The women there question the intention of the abbot or ascribe the good deed a sinful intent and, returning to the village, their tell the story to the villagers. The next day the befuddled villagers force the abbot into exile and, as a result, there were no clergymen left in the village. The abbot leaves cursing and goes to Nüsa village.

Gat-Aghpyur[23] [The Milk Fountain]

There is a fountain within a ten-minute walk southeast from the village. It is a semicircle-shaped fountain, half in ruins. There are many superstitions associated with this fountain. Near the fountain, a large rock has a grave-like ditch, which is said to be St. Anna's[24] grave. The water of Gat-Aghpyur is very cold and during the summer people from nearby places come specifically to drink its water. The fountain has an official day named after it, May 7. On that day all villagers, without exception, go to Gat-Aghpyur, taking along their cows, so that the cows increase their milk production. At noon, all Nirzetis go to the fountain accompanied by their priest, their teachers, and students. There they dedicate the *madagh* [sacrifice of an animal]. The students sing, brides and young girls dance, and children play various games. On that day Nirze is in total excitement, joy is everywhere. Sometimes women, who have recently given birth to boys and whose milk is insufficient or has stopped, go to Gat-Aghpyur or

---

23. The fountain is also known as Gatnaghpyur, a more literary form for the same word.
24. According to apocryphal Christian and Islamic traditions, St. Anna is the mother of Mary, and the grandmother of Jesus.

Gat-Aghpyur (earliest known photograph, from the 1960s; photographer unknown. Courtesy of Sinan Mordağ).

Chapter 1

send someone there to bring its water to wash their breasts and drink it to increase their milk.[25] Poor superstitions and inane thoughts. I should add that sometimes it does happen that there is an increase of milk, and that one incident becomes the reason for thousands to pursue that cure.

There are also young men who appear there on their horses to show off to the young girls. Those betrothed, or are about to be, even if in other towns, return for that day; will all the young women not be there dancing? And this way, the villagers dance and sing and enjoy the madagh until evening arrives and it is time to go to church. The women and young girls return home. And if seven drops of rain fall on that day, the school students go to church singing, knowing that the madagh has been accepted and there will be plentifulness that year.

The Hole Stone *[Dzag Kare]*

The Hole Stone is a big [square] rock which has a hole on its four sides, overlooking a vale nearly five minutes west of the village. Children who have difficulty sleeping are taken immediately to the Hole Stone and passed through the hole as a few prayers are said. As was the case with Gat Aghpyur, should it happen that a child ended up having a good sleep, then the miracle is considered to have occurred.

The Orphan Church (Öksüz Zham in Turkish) is a church-like structure sculpted inside a rock directly across from the village, between Gat Aghpyur and the Hole Stone. The story is told that a light, in the form of a lamp, emerges from the Hole Stone, moves to the Orphan Church, and then to Gat-Aghpyur… I lived in the village until I was nineteen years old, but failed to see such a light even once… And many others like me have failed to have such luck. The strange thing is that although no one had seen that light, the poor women believed this story to be true.

Nirze's position

As I have said, Nirze is situated in a dale and has beautiful stone houses which, for the most part, are connected to each other by their roofs, as well as by underground tunnels. In addition, within five to ten minutes of the

---

25. Vahan Kurkjian, a Nirzetsi the author will write about later in the book, has a somewhat more detailed description of this custom in a short article titled "Gatnaghpyur," in the periodical Pyuragn, (Bolis),1896, p. 360.

Hole Stone (a recent photo, unknown photographer).

village there are very wide, man-made caves where up to 2,000 people can find refuge. From the point of view of self-defense, Nirze is much better prepared than other surrounding villages. Alas, the people lack faith in themselves. Nirzetsis are ordinarily metalsmiths, cutlers, and textile workers. There are also shopkeepers and merchants among them. Hardly any Armenians work the land; the fields of Armenians are cultivated by Muslims. Most of the residents of the village belong to the middle class. Very few are rich, and there are no poor people. The people there are hospitable and fatalistic. The village has more gardens than wheat fields. These gardens and orchards surround the village on four sides. If you stand on a roof and look around, especially during spring, you would see green across a wide stretch of land, with apple, pear, apricot, plum, walnut, and other trees. By and large, every household has a vineyard or an orchard, so that there is no dearth of fruits when the time comes.

The Monday of Great Lent[26]

There is a custom in Nirze that is beautiful and at the same time pleasant to the youth of the village. All those who have had a wedding during the year will arrange for a second feast similar to the first on *Paregentan* [Shrovetide].

---

26. In the Armenian Apostolic Church, as in all Eastern Christian traditions, lent begins on Monday, and not Wednesday.

Chapter 1

The feasts are held on the roofs with the participation of both sexes. They dance and light wood fires, the flames of which rise very high, and they go around the fire dancing. After a few hours they come down into the house of the wedded to eat and drink and enjoy themselves until morning. The men, especially the young, will be so tired that it will be difficult for them to get up early enough to make it to church. That is why it was decided that there should be a house-by-house search for whoever among the men, rich or poor, is absent from church—may the Lord have mercy on them—and who would then be asked to choose among the following as punishment: (1) To mount a donkey backwards and hold his tail, (2) to be tied to a ladder and carried in the streets of the village, (3) To pay a penalty to the church, (4) to give gifts to each of those gathered in front of their house, or (5) bribe the leaders of the crowd. The subject must accept one of those conditions or else force will be used, and fights often break out. If one of those who failed to appear in church is captured, he is gagged, taken to his mother-in-law's house, and made to spend a lot of money.

The 1896 event in Nirze

As in other places, Nirze too was subjected to looting by a Turkish mob in 1896. The event must have been quite significant, although, having been too young, I do not remember any incident or personality. Relying on what was related later, I had heard that only five or ten homes, eye-catching homes, were looted, and a few were killed: I remember Yeghia Agha Aselbegian and Arabian Oghlu. Haji Hagop Aselbegian was not killed, but his feet had been pressed like *basturma* [spiced and cured beef], and it took him five to ten years to recover somewhat and start to walk a little with a limp. They say he also ended up with diminished mental capacity.

The reason that so few homes were looted and so few men killed is absolutely thanks to the Turks. Had it not been for them, the mob would have finished us all in a single day. It is said that some Turks picked up their guns and stood at the entrance of streets and swore that anyone who approached would be shot. And thus, they saved many districts.[27] They say that my father happened to come home that day from another place and

---

27. There are many cases where Turkish, Kurdish and other Muslim neighbors, sometimes collectively and more often individually, saved Armenians from the waves of massacres beginning in 1894.

brought an Afshar[28] with him. The villagers heard that a brave man had come to our home and they started gathering in our house and, as I mentioned before, there was no room to drop a pin in the house. I should have been able to write more about this, but as I said, I don't remember anything.

About the priest, once again

As I have said earlier, after the death of Der Stepan, Nirze did not have a resident priest. The village had temporary priests who came for a couple of months or couple of years. The villagers realized that this was an impossible situation and determined that a permanent priest was a necessity. The suggestion was made to have one of the villagers selected for the position. Let me say immediately, that I was in the United States by that time and I was informed of the details in a letter. Instead of relating the contents, I reproduce the letter here in full.

My dear and cherished[29] children
Senekerim and Vahan Effendis
Nirze, February 12, 1912

On Poon Paregentan [Shrovetide Sunday] we celebrated the betrothal of Haji Bey, may you have the same fortune, to the daughter of Maryan [Maryam?] Haji Sarkissian.

The Monday after Lent I went to church for fear of being forced to sit backwards on the donkey. A big fight broke out in the church. If you ask what was the reason, I will relate just the way it happened. A group of men were involved in the selection of a priest from among four candidates: Antreas, Yeghiazar, Simon Effendi, Aleksiyan Garabed.[30]

---

28. The Afshar are one of the Oghuz tribes originally from Central Asia who settled in what are today Iranian Azerbaijan, the Republic of Azerbaijan, and Eastern Turkey.
29. The Armenian word is *garodali*; it refers to someone who is missed very much.
30. This process of choosing a village priest raises many questions. Were they choosing from men with training and qualifications to become priests? From among their deacons? It is interesting that they are doing this on their own accord, without oversight from their local bishop or the Patriarchate, which assumed that they possessed or assumed such a degree of local autonomy to select their own priest from amongst their own community.

Chapter 1

The ones looking after this affair are Dr. Harutiune Bey, Mgrdich Effendi, Iki Keish Oghlu and Pakhleoghlu. All of them favored Antreas and wanted that voters be at least twenty-five years old. The opposing party wanted the minimum [voting] age to be fifteen, since they counted on the fact that the side supporting Antreas were all older, there were no fifteen-year-olds. A fight broke out in the church yard on this account. Everyone gathered in the House of God. Some did not accept the result of the voting because Andreas got thirty-four votes, whereas others [received] more than eighty. Although trustees were asked for an explanation, they did not give one. After many rounds of fighting like this, the crowd dispersed, but now they are looking for ways to come together and compromise. Let's see what will happen at the end.

Your father
Kheder Khederian

This is how the Nirze affair happened. Always partisanship and, as a result, always fights. Unfortunately, the work of the village suffers and nothing goes forward, as they always cross one another.

Khederian family, (Nirze, 1913, from the original Armenian edition, photographer unknown).

Chapter 2

The extended Khederian family

I said in Chapter One that Nirzetsis have come from a number of villages. Among them were the Khederians who came from the village of Derseah around 1765. The first of our ancestors was Kheder Agha. Unfortunately, I don't know any stories attached to his name. He was married to a daughter of Haji Khacherians, had four sons named Bal Agha, Sarkis, Garabed, Khacher, and two daughters, named Srpuhi and Yeghisapet. I will refer to their biographies on another occasion. Kheder Agha died at age ninety. [After his death] Their sons separated and the two daughters got married. Being the oldest, Bal Agha left the house and had a separate house built for himself. The other three sons divided the family house into three and settled there temporarily. Bal Agha bought an old house. When they were digging to lay the foundations on the ruins of the old house, a Turkish worker found a jug full of gold pieces. He grabbed it and disappeared. They searched for him but could not find him. In his time Bal Agha was one of the rich men, but he left no significant wealth when he died due to his excessive hospitality and spending. He had three sons, Hovhannes, Khacher and Sdepan; and two daughters, Maryam and Yeva.

The first son, Hovhannes, was a very smart and clever young man who knew Ottoman very well. As a consequence, he performed all the government's paperwork with his busy pen. But his life ended very early, at age twenty-one. The sad thing is that Hovhannes did not leave a memorable deed and the villagers do not mention his name, and it may be that they have never even heard of him. My respects to you, my dear uncle.

My father's life and death

As I have mentioned, Bal Agha had three sons and two daughters. After the death of his eldest, Hovhannes, he arranged for his youngest son, Kheder (my father), to marry Miss Yeva Haji Sarkissian, one of the daughters of a highly-respected family. My father had attended school for only a few years and learned part of the alphabet. But apparently my grandfather needed someone and took my father to his shop to work on the blower,[31] and thus

---

31. The Armenian expression is փուբ քաշել, *puk kashel*, literally "to draw wind."

he remained uneducated. But due to his cleverness my father learned how to read and write to the extent that he required (witness the letters he wrote to America). Thus, he did not need others to do his writing, and he got things done by his own hands. My father, like my grandfather, had perfected his trade. After my grandfather's death, the shop was left to my father, who by that time had three or four children and had taken the responsibility upon himself for a large family. He worked very hard and that sweat and blood produced only a modest result. He was extremely hospitable and did not like to have meals without guests. His workplace was in the Boghazlian area until 1897.

At that time my maternal uncle was sought by the government as a revolutionary and was unemployed. So, being responsible for two families, my father left his old job and went to Gharajaviran, a Greek village, where he had already arranged for a shop, and stayed there for ten years tirelessly [with my uncle]. Sometimes my uncle was taken to jail and tortured. But this too did not last, as my uncle returned having benefitted from Sultan Hamid's amnesty. My uncle's main fault was his alcoholism. For that reason, my father split from him, and after working in various villages and towns, finally settled in the Turkish village named Yelderem. That is the village where my father took me. Yelderem was a village that its neighbors dubbed Kuchuk Msr [Little Egypt]. We finally settled there and opened a grocery store. First my brother left for Bolis and the shop was left to the joint management of a Turk and myself. And when I too departed, everything was left on my father's shoulders.

I asked my father that he leave everything and return home. My father accepted my recommendation. I sent him as much money as he requested. But, alas, in addition to failing to perform his filial duties, my brother also plotted against him. Directly or indirectly, he led my father to believe that as his eldest son, my father should give him an IOU worth 100 or 200 gold liras. My father absolutely refused. So, my brother stopped sending letters and money, and he instructed our relatives in Nirze to give as much trouble to my father as possible until he got what he wanted.

Since I heard about this treachery, father, I have been thinking about it day and night; sometimes I weep. At the end, the question remained unresolved. My mother had already died. My uncle and others tried to convince my father to get married again. But my father knew that I was his

Chapter 2

sole source of income, so it was necessary to ask and obtain my opinion. My brother Baruyr heard about this and was altogether against this new development. He wrote me the following letter.

Nirze, November 14, 1911

Honorable Sen[ekerim] and Vah[an] Khederian

Dear brothers,

I cannot tell you how happy I was when I received your letter a week ago. But I should tell you that the moment the letter arrived Mr. Hagopjan, thought to be my father's letter writer, took the letter and did not read it in our presence. He read it in a separate place, but later we came to know everything. I read your letter and was informed of your opinion. You know, dear brother, my uncle has written to you so that you give your consent to our father's marriage. But I hope you have refused. They are not making this proposition thinking of our progress and welfare, but rather they are our internal enemies, who will watch and laugh at us; they are doing this for their own gain. But you should know that if our father gets married, something that is in our hands, our dispersion will be inevitable. Immediately after I will kill myself, and you will be subjected to many more losses. Therefore, we appeal to you to do what you can. Dear brothers, do not forget your fatherland, and plan to return soon. Also, do not do whatever my uncle asks of you.

If my father gets his way, our situation will be untenable. Please write from that perspective and ask him not to open his mouth again, otherwise we will be the laughing stock of the village. I will share with you those letters as the truth, you can decide whatever you want. My paternal aunt and my sister weep all day wandering "whether they will see Senekerim and Vahan."

As for me, if you are going to return to this country, please make sure you send me to a monastery, but don't forget to bring me a watch and a pistol. But if you will not be returning, let me know so that I get there too. I wish to see your faces, nothing else. Don't spare the money you send. Please also send your photographs. Others send their photographs, but you have not sent any to date. How expensive could that be? Our teacher has written you a letter and you have not responded. Will you answer this letter in detail?

Respectfully
Your own brother
Baruyr Khederian

After reading this letter I immediately wrote to my father, but in the meantime a letter had arrived from my father as well, asking our consent for his marriage, and I answered in the following manner:

Dear father, you are past fifty-five years of age, and I am sure you have listened to others. Think first and then take your steps. The decision is yours; do as you wish. I am ready to help you until the end of my life, even more than necessary.

After receiving my letter, my father put an end to the discussion; he left the store and started roaming around the villages. But as I said, my brother did not leave him alone. The poor man got so disturbed by these worries that he fell prey to a thousand-and-one illnesses.

In his August 26, 1912 letter, my father said, "I am extremely satisfied with your fulfilling of your filial responsibilities," "selam para kelam para" [Turkish saying, "A greeting costs (is) money, a word is money," i.e., everything costs money]

And then one day I received the following letter.

November 18, 1913, Nirze
My wise, beloved, and sincerely missed brother Senekerim Effendi Khederian,

We are extremely happy to receive your letter dated November 18, although we are sad with regard to one aspect; it is God's imperative, we could not do anything. May God grant you [a long] life and keep you away from all grief, amen. Senekerim Effendi, you had wanted some information in your letter. Your letter reached before the illness of the deceased, whose name is eternal and precious, beloved father of all of us, may his soul rest in peace.

First it started like a flu in his throat. We waited two or three months [hoping] for an improvement. Then, winter arrived and that time he started to have pain in his throat. He passed his time in this

Chapter 2

situation until Lent. It got worse. A swelling occurred under his chin. It was hard like iron. We had Khachig Effendi inspect it, he came five or six times, but finally he gave up hope and said [your father] would die. Later, we decided to go to Talas. Yeghyazar Agha, Mgrdich Effendi all together went to Talas and I went to Kayseri. They came to Kayseri in the evening. We slept over there. I stopped by Mgrdich Effendi and asked what the old man had said. When he replied "What shall I say? Your heart would get heavy." My heart ached. He started to tell the news. There was no way out. He had been secretly informed that the bump should not be taken out. If it had been removed a bigger one would have appeared in its place. "Do not cause pain in vain. He will live for three months and die in the fourth" he said. "Let me tell you why this happens", he added. "When someone has something in his heart, joy or grief, or a problem that he cannot express due to shame, this is the cause [of this disease]." In fact, he died after three months, just as he had said. There are many more things that cannot be explained by writing. We had Aslanian inspect him but he could not save him either. They said it was syphilis.[32] We went to Soorp Garabed for fifteen days. He got much better, but suddenly he worsened and left us. May God grant you [long] life. Don't worry, you have done your duties as a son. There was nothing more that you could do. May God grant you your wishes.

There is another good thing. He had received your news before he died and was delighted. He even spent Garabed Effendi's seven or eight gold liras in a short time. Garabed Effendi received such a favor. If he had not done this favor it would have been a burden on his heart until his death. This is also from God. Anyway, I cannot write long, excuse me. But I also want to write you about this issue of fifteen gold liras. He had taken a portion of it from Nekdaritsa by the exchange of a note. We bought some flour and four or five hampers of hay, donated one gold lira to the church, spent two or three gold liras to meet some small needs. Three gold liras went to Artin Effendi. Still, there is a debt of one gold lira to be paid to him. Let me itemize all one by one later. I cannot recall [now] for what else it has been spent. I think there will remain a debt of one or two gold liras. We could not buy enough flour. We bought only *fifty batmans [750 lbs.] because we could not dare to spend more money*

---

32. It is more likely that the patient had laryngeal cancer.

lest Senekerim Effendi not accept it and we may have a big problem then. Thank you for allowing to spend it but the time has passed [to buy more flour]. Never mind.

I hope you are rewarded by God for your humanity. Your goodness has reached heaven. There is no other sorrow here. Everybody is well and peaceful. They eat, drink, and pray. You also asked to whom you should bequeath your house, worrying that if you commend it any one person, the others may feel offended. Please do not worry about me. Whomever you commend I will advise and help them as much as I can if they come to me and ask for my advice and help. I shall not abandon you, but if you abandon [me] I will not chase and force you to cooperate with me. If you could imagine my workload you would be surprised. I tend to the needs of three fourths of our village. Even those households that have their men forward all their needs to me: "We need this much flour, that much wheat." I cannot refuse them; I promise to do my best. I am extremely pleased with you. I wish you eternal health and wellbeing my dear.

Hagopjan S. Chelebjian

My father died, but I have no regret of any kind, because I have fully discharged my filial responsibilities. In his April 25, 1911 letter my father says, "When I received your letter, it included a check for twenty-one Ottoman gold liras. I took it to Gesaria and cashed it. But I cried when counting it, thinking, how much blood and sweat Senekerim must have shed …"

My mother's life and death

(The letters of my aunt, sister, and mother)

My mother got married when she was around sixteen years old. Yet she was surprisingly clever and gifted with numbers. She was obedient to her husband and had a peaceful and love-filled life. Coming from a wealthy family, she should have been a delicate and pretentious girl. But, on the contrary, she was as tough and hardworking after she got married as she was tough and active when a young girl. She used to say that "my father had flocks of sheep, may be one to two thousand, and to milk them I walked daily for about half an hour to a place called Ayros, where there

Chapter 2

were specially-prepared sheep folds. In addition to sheep, there were also mules, horses, cows, etc."

My grandfather had sufficient servants, who were also cared for by my mother. It is due to that hard work that after a few years she was content to engage in textile work, and in this way she helped my father and satisfied her need for physical work. Her life was stormy. Hardly thirty-five years old, she looked forty-five. The reason? Her youngest and dearest brother, Haji Boghos, was pursued by the Ottoman authorities because he was a member of one of the revolutionary organizations. Every other day the house would be surrounded. Turkish officials would torture the members of the household as best as they could. As the sister of the person being sought, my mother, was among those affected.

That situation continued for five to ten years. One day twenty or thirty policemen surround the house again. After a very thorough search, in order not to return empty-handed, they arrested my mother and my aunt and put them in jail in Gesaria. At that time my brother Vahan was nine months old, so he too was taken to jail. But as soon as he heard about it, my father posted bail and arranged for their release.

As I have mentioned before, having been subject to general amnesty, my uncle returned from Egypt. But any time a crime or theft occurred they would arrest my uncle as an old revolutionary, and during such confinements he would be tortured Turkish-style. My mother witnessed all of these, and you know, of course, how a sister cherishes a brother. My mother was then so affected by the Turkish savagery that eventually she ended up with an incurable disease that worsened every time her brother was jailed. So, she spent most of her life being sick. Doctor Khachig Effendi Doevletian, who was our family doctor, conscientiously provided my mother care. He would often refuse payment for his visit. My mother was tall, big-boned and strong, with large black eyes, beautiful eyebrows, black hair, and an attractive face.

In recent times my mother completely withdrew from her work, leaving house chores to my paternal aunt. My mother had seven children. The first died, the others, five boys and one girl, are still alive. The boys are named Garabed, Senekerim, Vahan, Baruyr and Sarkis. My sister's name is Nigdar. My aunt was the one who raised all of them. That is why we all remember her name with gratitude and respect. My mother was an

Haji Boghos family, (Nirze, from the original Armenian edition, photographer unknown).

Nusa Girls School, 1 May 1913 (from the original Armenian edition, photographer unknown).

Chapter 2

Osmantsi [Ottoman], as they say: liberal, truthful and shy. She was extremely hospitable, so that whoever the guest—bey, pasha or common mortal, Armenian or not—they were all honored equally. She did not like to have dinner with family members alone; she would wait until a guest showed up. My mother was an azkaser [nation-loving] person.[33] When a beggar appeared at the door asking for alms, my aunt, who was a little stingy, would give some bread or bulghur [cracked wheat]. But my mother would scold her and would instruct that the beggar be given more than the minimum. In 1905-1906 she became seriously ill; the poor woman had a broken heart. The love she had for her brother led her to that state. She was in bed for around two years. The doctor indicated signs of hopelessness, or led the family to realize indirectly that there was no hope for recovery.

Summer came and we were compelled to go to the shop to make a living. But neither my father nor any of us could really function. We were overtaken by a kind of weakness, hopelessness. One day my paternal uncle Stepan walked in unexpectedly and demanded that my father go home. We knew what my uncle was signaling. We were all silent and could not ask why our father was needed at home. We were afraid it might have something to do with our mother. But what was done was done, what could we do? Without saying a word, my father got on his horse at lightning speed and then said, "Children, you stay here, I will be back tomorrow."

But who had the heart to wait? A mother's death is made known and a son stays in a village seven or eight hours away? Vahan and I decided to walk all night and make it at least to the funeral of our mother, maybe, although our father and uncle had told us strictly that we should stay where we were. We feigned obedience, but inside we were troubled. Finally, Vahan and I started out on the road. We needed eight hours to get home.

---

33. The Armenian expression is ազգասէր, *azkaser* (*azk-a-ser*), literally "nation-loving." When used by Armenians, the term "nation" in the Ottoman Empire refers to the larger Armenian people or community, a formally recognized non-Muslim ethno-religious group. Nation-loving refers to someone who cared about, and participated in Armenian community institutions—usually the church, schools, charities, elected assemblies—that ran the affairs of the ethno-religious group. The term azk could mean, interchangeably, community or people. Later the term azk referred to the nation only.

We had no horses or donkeys to ride, all had been taken. We had to walk. It was to be so difficult, oh God! But no, the love of mother and duties of a child do not allow for absence, even if it will be her final hour.

Oh, the evening of that march. Were we walking or running? I don't know. At moments I would cry, remembering like a child the doting that I had enjoyed months earlier. But I did not want to tell Vahan about the pain that so floored me. So, I wiped the tears in my eyes away from him. I wanted to say something, to console him. I felt that he too was weeping like me, but words were dying on my lips, I could say nothing. We continued on our way. Sometimes I felt strength in me to set aside my pain and sorrow with the faint hope that my mother is not dead, that the call had come because she is seriously ill. Still, no guessing could comfort me, the event itself was inconsolable. After eight hours of tortuous road, we finally reached the orchards near Nirze without having exchanged a single word.

By midday we could see the houses. I wondered if we might come across anyone who might have some news of our mother. I looked around. I could see some figures moving in the orchards. I decided to go to them and ask. But then I stopped, for perhaps what I might hear would be bad news. What would be our state, especially that of poor Vahan; tears were running down his eyes. I noticed that familiar people who saw us would turn their faces away and did not show any indication that they wanted to talk. I sensed that there was something. I started to walk at a distance when I saw people. Perhaps I was about to hear the bad, tragic news.

We finally arrived in awe and fear. As a child I had run up and down our street a thousand times; now it seemed that it took many minutes to take each step, so slow was our advance. Those who saw us in the street would change their route. I felt the horror of what had happened. I could not say even one word. My God, what was this silence! Although silent, the faces of everyone we met seemed to be saying, "Poor boy, why did you come? You are too late, you did not get here soon enough to say goodbye, to hear your mother say goodbye. Poor, poor boy." The stones were speaking those words, the grass was conveying the news. Even the pavements seemed to be murmuring "Two days ago they took your mother by trampling all over us to where you can never see her again." Everything around us was speaking. Yet, without losing hope, we continued walking to our beloved paternal hearth. Even our trees, whose branches heated the water of the dead, began to protest … Damn you trees, for having produced wood to heat the water, damn you pavement, which allowed our dear mother's coffin to be taken over you.

We finally reached our door. Our house has two doors: one on the western side and the other on the southeastern. We tried to enter from the latter. And what did we see? A huge crowd had followed us, without our knowledge: relatives, neighbors, friends, all coming to our house. Of course, with the purpose of consoling us. I did not wait for them. I entered; I did not even look at Vahan. Suddenly I felt joy when I realized that there was no one in the hallway of the house, there were no lights, and for a moment I thought that is not how a house with a dead person in it would be, which meant my mother was alive. I rushed up the ten or fifteen flights of stairs to greet my dear mother. Alas, I fell on the floor, unconscious. When I woke up I observed that my mother's bed and health-related objects had been taken out of the room and only guests were left. They all had words of consolation. I cried for two three days and only then was I able to reconcile myself to the situation.

This is how I lost my mother. But her progeny stand strong and remember her name with respect. Dear mother, we are in America today. And when tomorrow the opportunity arises to visit our homeland again, we will prostrate again by your grave with deep yearning.

My respect to your memory, dear mother.

My paternal aunts

I have two aunts, Maryam and Yeva. Maryam was married at eighteen to an honorable, kind, and wealthy young man named Haji Hagop Haji Khacherian. They had three boys and a daughter. One of their sons, Asdur, was slaughtered like a sheep in Bolis in 1896 by the wild Turks. The youngest, Harutiune, was a tall, educated young man without a peer in the village; he married at age twenty-four. Harutiune, who was afflicted with an incurable disease, passed away shortly after his thirty-fifth birthday. My aunt married off her daughter and the son-in-law came to live with them, adding one more source of pain to ours.

My aunt Yeva married a handsome young merchant, Garabed Gederian, who did business in Bolis. Two years after their marriage Garabed went to live in Bolis to take charge of his business but fate did not allow him to live for long. The news of his death, sometime around 1887, struck my aunt like lightning. They had two children. The older was a boy, Antranig, and the second a girl, Yeghisapet. So, my aunt Yeva too was compelled to move to our house.

That is why my mother felt comfortable not concerning herself with home chores. My aunts were always helping her. When I came to America, each letter I sent expressed my gratitude to them. I love them as my mother. They are the ones who raised me and my brothers and we owe our health to them.

My sister

My sister was a lady of elegant appearance, with black eyes, black hair, and medium height. At fourteen years of age she was engaged to a respectable young man by the name of Garabed Müdürian. They were married after nearly three years of engagement. To date they have four children. After my mother's death my sister ended up with all of her household duties. As separate as their household was, she was always taking care of us. She came by every morning, without exception, gave instructions, and left. She became an extremely conscientious and good-hearted woman. She never wanted to stay still for a minute when she was a girl. After sharing equally the household chores with my aunts, she would also weave rugs. She worked so fast and cleverly that her rugs were admired by others; in this way, she contributed significantly to the expenses of the household. She was a great economizer, she spent at the right time and at the right place. She was obedient to her husband and mother-in-law. She had three chubby children: Hovhannes, Yeghisapet, and Rafael. The first, my God, he was such a fiery-eyed, ruddy-cheeked adolescent of medium height. Judging from his personality and movements you would think he was twenty years old. How I loved Hovhannes, I never felt contented unless I saw him each day. Still, just as is the case with many others, we have not had any news from them for two years now.

Yeghisapet was an angel with blonde hair, blue eyes, and a red and white face. Everyone who saw her admired her beauty. But now the sickle of the vile Turk has mowed her, too. I wonder if I will see her again. She would cross my path each day after school and we would walk home, joking. I used to carry them [three children] as cherished ones up the stairs.

Chapter 2

When one recalls these memories, can one still be left with the desire to suffer in this land of bantukhds [migrant or itinerant workers]?

Rafael was born after I had left for America, so I have no information about him.

My sister loved us equally. But she had a special love for, and faith in me. When I came to America I would often receive letters from her. I am reproducing one of them in full as an example of the expression of her sincere love for me.

> *November 1, 1911 Nirze*
> *My Beloved Brother Senekerim Effendi,[34]*
>
> *I received your letter a few days ago and it made me extremely happy and joyful. "They name the rose a violet, I could not attain my wishes in this world, I am searching for my lost sibling."[35] Senekerim, I trust you are healthy. If you are well, may you return to your home one day. "May the nightingale not tweet in high pitches, [not even] my enemy's brother should be gone for five years." "The [ceiling of the] palace of America is high, Don't stay long for little money, Don't forget your cherished fellow townspeople and home." "In my thoughts during daytime, In my dreams at night, In my glass while drinking water, In my spoon while eating." My dear brother, know that this is how [much] I am longing for you. "Months are passing, years are not. Separation is not endurable at this young age." My beloved Senekerim Effendi, you should come [home] this year so that Vahan can come next year. We will do your engagement during Christmas, let me know which of the girls I mentioned you prefer. Don't neglect to write.*
>
> *Mrs. Nekdaritsa Müdürian.*

My sister had a wish. In almost every letter she sent me since I arrived in the United States, she would write, "My dear brother, allow me to arrange for your engagement." Apparently, while still in the crib, I was engaged (beshig kertmesi) [beşik kertmesi in Turkish, or cradle notching], and my sister demanded that my mother's promise be kept. But, unfortunately, I gave a negative reply in each case. Not because I did not like the girl, but

---

34. This letter is written in Turkish, using the Armenian alphabet.
35. Obviously an attempt at poetry or use of sayings, of which the letter is full.

because I wanted to secure my future. My sister had misunderstood me and this time she sent the photos of three or four girls with biographical details, which I do not desire to make public. But I will place here one of her letters just to show how eager my sister was to see me engaged.

April 23, 1912 Nirze[36]
My Beloved and Missed Brother Senekerim Khederian,

First of all, let me ask about your well-being which is delicate as a rose. I hope you do not have any troubles.

I received your letter two weeks ago and it made me very happy. We also received the photograph you sent. People grabbed it from one another's hands. I speak to your image, but it does not reply. There is no remedy for separation. If you ask about the situation here, Turkey has no order, as you know, my brother, whom I miss. Say "hello" to your brother-in-law and little Vahan. Our fate is cloudy here, give your blessings anyway. What a pity that I cannot write. I want to write letters full of my wishes. My grieving brothers, my rosy skin has turned pale since you left. Your mother left you as a blessing for me, let's keep your blessings with me, my dear. When you went down the hill of our hometown, got on the horse, and left for foreign lands, I thought my soul had left my body. I became separated from you, I turned into an outsider, I have burned for you, turned into ashes.

My beloved brother Senekerim, you wrote in your previous letter that we should never talk to you about girls. I wrote three or four times before, and I am writing again. If you ask why, [it is] not to let a foreign girl enter our family. While others are seeking [girls to marry] from corner to corner, why should we give the one girl now in our hands to strangers? You say soldiership [probably meaning bachelorship] is killing you. If you marry this girl, you will be saved from soldiership. They came from Munjusun, from the city and other places, to ask for her hand. I did not allow that [to go through]. They came from rich cities to ask [for her hand], Mgrdich Effendi promised [her hand] but I did not permit it. The brute says that he will not let her go to the foreign lands; he says he would give her to his uncle's son. Dear brother, do not think of her as you remember. She has become such a girl that if you saw her with your

---

36. This letter too is in Turkish and written with the Armenian alphabet.

own eyes you would immediately say "yes". If you think I am lying, ask travelers [coming from here]. The girl is still young. Stay there two or three [more] years, later you may come with Armenak to marry her. I request from here, please do not turn me down before the eyes of everyone. I will betroth you, whether you accept it or not, act accordingly. I will wait for the reply to this letter.

Mrs. Nekdaritsa Müdürian

My sister's interest was not only in getting me engaged. Her aim was to make it easy for me to return, as she feared that I might be stuck in this land forever, or return very late. But alas, she was unable to achieve her goal. The new arrivals relate that my sister would go to see any one in Nirze who was going to come to America and ask them, in tears, that they convey to me her wishes and requests. Neither her wishes, nor her requests were realized. Our plans were nullified. The future is just about destroyed and to a large degree, I have turned hopeless. My sister, who used to write such beautiful and yearning letters, which I would read in tears, is no more. My sister, who yesterday used to send gifts with travelers and which I once enjoyed, is lost. Finally, the one who used to labor hard for a better future for me is no longer. What a sorrowful change. Now it is I who is worried, with this uncertain present and bitter future. Who knows on which mountain the Turkish vipers killed her, or in what harem she may be imprisoned. Do not despair, my sister, in return for your caring of yesterday we possess our love and yearning for you. Soon we will see the day when we will be able to breathe freely, and we will come to join you.

You have not forgotten us.
And we will not forget you.

My paternal uncles and their lives

I have written in the previous pages that the Khederian clan established itself in Nirze in 1765, had children by the names of Bal Agha, Sarkis, Garabed and Khacher. We have said what there was to be said about Bal Agha already. Now it is Sarkis's turn. Sarkis Emmi [uncle in Turkish] was a God-fearing, sociable, Christian, and independent old man. Since he had no knack for any trade, his brothers thought it more appropriate to buy him a few pairs of oxen and a few acres of land and have him work the land. This white-haired old man had two daughters, Yeghisapet and Srpuhi. Yeghisapet married Garabed Agha Pavliyan, and the younger daughter Srpuhi wedded Garabed Haji Khacherian. Not having any boys, Khacherian, who had come to live in his wife's household, left his daughters and wife and disappeared for some twenty years. Srpuhi raised her children with the sweat of her brow. The older daughter, clever and energetic, wove carpets, and they earned their daily keep with ease. The old man, Sarkis, died when he was seventy-five years old, leaving considerable wealth, a house, orchards, etc.

Unfortunately, I have not been able to gather much information on Garabed Khederian, except that being dainty and slender, he was sent to Bolis to go into business. Garabed Emmi had two children, one boy and one girl, Serovpe and Yeghisapet. Yeghisapet was married to Hagop Agha Haji Bedrossian. Serovpe was married to Makruhi Müdürian. Makruhi Müdürian was a gentle and virtuous woman. Although her husband was irritable, she was serious and patient. They had six or seven children but a few died and only one boy and two girls survived: Garabed, Veronica and … Nature did not allow them to have a peaceful life. After the death of the children, I heard that Makruhi also passed away following a brief illness, leaving behind small children.

Her cousin Serovpe was an ironsmith. He was a nervous man and cursed a lot. When angry, he did not spare even friends and family. He had a stormy life. Recently he sent one of his sons, Garabed, to America, while he, sensing that he had committed too many sins against the Lord, traveled to Jerusalem to beg for forgiveness and at the same time earned the very desirable title of mahdesi.[37]

Khacher Khederian, a polite and educated young man, received his education in Gesaria, if I am not mistaken, and was a teacher in Nirze for some five or six years. Then he went to Bolis and delved in sculpture. So, he had a very peaceful and comfortable life. The only tragic event had been that while an adolescent he lost two fingers that were crushed under a stone. Khacher Emmi was married to… and lost his wife after having a daughter and married a second time, to Nazlu Abajian. Nazlu Abajian,

---

37. Mahdesi, derived from the Arabic *muqdisi*, a Jerusalemite, or someone who has been to Jerusalem on a pilgrimage, the same haji. It is possible that mahdesi is a more venerable term than haji.

who was physically large, was an energetic and clever lady, the likes of whom one cannot find easily. They had one son and five daughters. The daughter from Khacher Emmi's first wife married my maternal uncle, Mr. Boghos Haji Sarkissian. His other children are named Yeranitsa, …, Zabel, Yeghisapet and Hayganush. Having quite a bit of money, Khacher Emmi returned to the village so that he might enjoy a quiet retirement. Because of the young age of their son, Garabed, they could not do any work and their money ran out quickly. Khacher died at the age of sixty or sixty-five. The burdens of the household were left to the very young Garabed, who left school and became a cutler. Fortunately, the girls came of age quickly and started working, and the family earned a livelihood. They had orchards, gardens, and a house. Is it possible to imagine how inconsolable was the state of these delicate girls who had not seen the face of the sun. The news reaching us could drive us… mad.

[About me] From my birth to the present day

They say that I was very shy as a child, having difficulty learning to read and write. Others my age made progress, while I could not even master A and B. But I did not remain in that situation for long. I flung down the problems of the weak-minded; at ages ten to twelve, I attacked my books with all my heart and spirit. In a few years I not only surpassed my age group but also my classmates, occupying close to first place in my school. This reversal happened during the time of our teachers G. Aselbegian, and later Srabian, under whose wing I learned a good deal of Ottoman.

Then came Mr. Hagop Hajenlian, a graduate of Soorp Garabed Monastery. He had hardly completed his studies when he was invited to teach in Nirze; he was paid twenty-four Ottoman gold liras a year, which was increased gradually. Mr. Hagop was endowed with many talents. The first year he paid extraordinary attention to the students, and in one year he taught students what took four years for other teachers to do. Our group of students of the fifth grade occupied an exceptional place in the school. Mr. Hagop spent almost half his time with us. Because we loved to learn in the evenings, we went to his room for special lessons, as if we were the privileged ones. I cannot forget that once only, he gave me a good beating on my soles, the *falakhga* [falakha, bastinado], for no reason at all. On another day he punished us for not having studied our lesson by making us stand at the door of the church.

His enthusiasm ebbed during the second year. The villagers became aware of the change. They warned him many times, saying "take care of your responsibilities," but Mr. Hagop remained indifferent. That produced a revolt; there were even attempts by the students to beat him up. I did not agree with them but remained silent out of fear of my friends. Since the attempts were fruitless, many students started losing interest in the school, except for me. I felt even more enthusiastic than before. Of the five students in the class, I was the only one left still attending lessons. The villagers also did not want the teacher, but because the agreement was for the whole year, they were compelled to keep him another eight months. During this period, he tried to teach me as much as possible within his capabilities, at the expense of the others.

In fact, it was a pleasure for teachers to work with me because I was diligent and advanced, and endowed with a sharp memory. As I have said, I satisfied my strivings by winning prizes like a hero. Twice I won the prize at the annual examinations. I have also won prizes at the regularly-held exams. I was admired for my observations during class. I was deficient in French; I had no desire to learn that language. In mathematics I was as advanced as the instruction of the school permitted. I studied more than what was demanded of me in history. I was successful almost equally in the other subjects. The only unfortunate thing was the absence of practical music. It was my deepest wish to learn to play an instrument. I had the impression that without music an education was defective.

One of the undeniable benefits I received from Mr. Hagop was that when I was the only student left in our class, he gave me more time than was allotted and during the evenings too I studied Turkish law, Muslim literature, and other courses in which I became adequately knowledgeable.

Alas, the eight months passed too quickly and my plans remained unfulfilled.

One of our rooms had been converted to a kind of den where neighbors gathered, especially during winter nights, and exchanged stories form the Old and New Testaments.

One way or the other after many arguments my teacher departed and was replaced by a new one, Khachig Effendi (from Tomarza). I went to school the first day and found out that, although a graduate from our monastery, he was not familiar with the books that we had been using.

Chapter 2

Thus, I was compelled to quit school. My father and brother suggested that I go to Soorp Garabed, but I refused to do so, the idiot that I was. Next I refused to go to Talas College. My constant reason was that I knew enough Armenian. But my father did not give up. He started working through others. At the end, unable to resist my aunt and her daughter, who were insisting upon it, I did promise to enter the monastery and come out a *vartabed* [celibate priest]. Everyone was happy, because that way there would be someone from our large family to intercede for the departed to easily enter the heavenly kingdom.

Negotiations with the director of the seminary, through M. Effendi Müdürian, had concluded and I was to be accepted tuition free when suddenly one of our relatives, Zabenian Agha Baba, visited us. I told him about my plan and he got very angry and called it an absolutely stupid move. "I am telling you, my son," he told me, "there is no money in being a *vartabed*. Let's talk of *martabed*.[38] Do you want to be a martabed in the future? Go overseas, Europe or America, don't get married, don't even think about it. Don't ever become a clergyman."

Encouraged by this kind of advice, I stubbornly refused to follow through the plan. My father threatened to give me to any tradesman as an apprentice, but he disregarded his threat in view of my young age.

My sister used to weave rugs in the house and I was designated an assistant to her on a temporary basis. But alas, that enjoyable period did not last long, as I was transferred again, this time to assist my father. He really did not need me, since he had more than one assistant. Regardless, the second year did prove to be a time when I was of some help. We later had a grocery shop under my oldest brother's management. One day we heard that he had left for Bolis without informing anyone. I was next in line to manage [the store] and I partnered with a Turk. That lasted only six months as suddenly I received a letter from my brother in America: he was insisting that I go there too. I had hardly gotten used to my work, when once again I undertook a long journey and went away from home.

I should not forget to mention that during this whole period I had nothing to do and could not have anything to do with beys and aghas.

---

38. This is a play on words. *Vartabed* means, literally, "Leader of education," or "Leader of work." *Martabed* is an alliteration, meaning "Leader of men."

To America

Before I received my brother's letter, my father sent someone after me to ask that I spend Easter vacation with them and to personally discuss some gossip that was circulating about me. I refused to go, using shop business as an excuse. But a month later the same contact, Garabed Torossian, came after me. It was he who brought me the letter from my brother. It was difficult to leave the village, but I could not resist my brother's insistence. I related the issue to my friend who commiserated with me but I had to comply.

I said my last goodbyes to my friends and left for the village. There was much commotion in our house; all was made ready for the trip [to America]. May 6 was the day of departure. The next day, May 7, is Nirze's official Feast Day. But I could not stay behind. Relatives and friends had already surrounded us. There was eating and drinking. Joy was everywhere. At 7 o'clock of the final day, when we were about to leave, Father Karekin, who was presiding over the table, filled his glass with wine and said, "My dear son, today is your last day at your patriarchal hearth. In a little while you will leave for a place unfamiliar to you. I trust in your love for your parents and your obedience. I have a modest piece of advice which you should never forget: try to be the master of your health, and then your money. Don't stay less than three or more than five years. At least don't forget your parents' tears…"

The feast ended with well wishes and opinions, and the procession headed for Nirze's famous spring, where some 200 people were assembled. When I was passing through the door I found the house empty, so I said goodbye to the walls. The carriage was waiting for me; I could not walk because I was exhausted as the result of sleeplessness. Whatever remained of the night I spent alone, in my bed, overtaken by unending thoughts. I remembered my mother, that wonderful soul, who had left us two years earlier. Slowly I remembered the caring and support I had enjoyed from her. What would her situation be if she was still alive today? I would have been happy if I had a last chance to kiss her hand; I was satisfied by shedding a few tears at her gravesite. I satisfied my yearning for my parents by having a warm cry in my father's arms. My friends had already left, so I had to hurry. For a moment, disregarding every thought of weakness in my

Chapter 2

mind, I dismounted from the carriage and walked with the crowd. The students from the school were singing appropriate songs. We proceeded across the village with the *"Hrashapar."* This was the last moment, there was no end to the kisses planted on my forehead. So warm was the kiss from my caring sister.

After giving some tips to the church sexton and students, the carriage moved. Where to? My father and a few friends accompanied me all the way to Gesaria. Traveling with me were my friends Garabed Kehyayan and Haig Abajian. In six or seven days we reached Mersin. Due to some currency issues, we stayed there for four days. We were supposed to reach America via Italy. After passing through towns and villages we reached Alexandria, and after two days in that city we left for Naples, one of Italy's historic cities, which was filled with electric lights. We stayed in a clean hotel in that city for five or six days. All expenses were paid by the ship company. A sizable army of Armenian swindlers had nested there, but we were free from them.

From Naples we reached New York in twelve days. I had travel notes but unfortunately lost them. I will try to write down roughly the basic points. After Naples I felt miserable and refused to eat or drink. Because of my illness I had trusted my money to Kehyayan. But when we were landing on Ellis Island we lost each other. So I was left without any money. After waiting for two days, I received some money from my brother and left for Watertown.

I arrived in Watertown at 4 pm on Saturday, June 15, 1910. After resting for two days, I started working at the Hood Rubber plant. This lasted for two days. I injured my hands and was obligated to leave that job. I was taken back to work on June 20 and this time had a position in the packing room working nights, a position I hold to date.

Corruption had become a major disease for some men who secured jobs. They were all Armenians, without exception. For between five and fifty dollars, they would secure you a job. One such man was my former teacher, Hagop Hajnlian, who occupied a leading position among them. I had heard about him and had hopes that instead of treating me as he did others he would take better care of me. I was mistaken. For twenty-five dollars I got a good job. It was not what he did that affected me in a negative way, but the phenomenon itself. What had happened to my former idealistic teacher, who now swam all day in the dirty pipe of materialism?

I had some successes in the factory and I owe them to him. During changes in the job, I encountered some unbrotherly jealousies, and so many times I was close to losing my job. Up to now I have worked nights and in that I have not found any inconvenience. My financial position has not been enviable, but I have enjoyed very good health. A year and a half into my job at the factory my older brother Vahan and I had a disagreement, and we separated. That became the justification for my brother to break all relations with our parents. As a result, the responsibility of helping our parents rested on my shoulders alone. But that was no reason to be discouraged. I have supported them, and will continue to do so until the last day of my life. Any money I saved I sent to my father. In case I came up short I borrowed money with interest and sent it to them. The total amount of money I sent was 198 Ottoman gold liras, or $902.95. In addition to not sending any money, my brother found different ways bring himself trouble. Brotherly ties do not allow me to publish these problems. Except that hearing about these things in the homeland, they sent a letter to my older brother....

During this period of troubles with my brother, many friends and companions advised me not to send all my savings to my parents because in the future I would be penniless. They also counseled that I reconcile with my brother so that he would help support our parents. I received many letters on this matter.

A letter from my maternal uncle Haji Boghos is very interesting in this respect, and I shall quote some segments.

December 11, 1911, Nirze[39]
Intelligent Senekerim Beg[40] *Khederian,*
My much-missed nephew Senekerim, I hear of your good fame and feel happy. I have a request from you considering the current situation, which you should accept. Christmas will arrive before this letter of mine reaches you. Please go to your brother at Christmas and wish him a

---

39. This letter is in Turkish, using the Armenian alphabet.
40. Turkish honorific, the same as bey.

Chapter 2

Merry Christmas. Even if your brother is bad, both of you were born from my sister. You should not be enemies. My dear nephew Senekerim, you are smart, but consider what happened to your [maternal] uncle and then make a decision in the service of God. Otherwise, it is vain even if your profit amounts to the [level of the] water of Kızılırmak [Halys River]. Do not take offense at these writings of mine, it is your decision anyway. After considering what I lived through, I wrote this letter to give you an idea. I wish everlasting health to you. All the family members ask about your health and well-being.

Your maternal uncle,

Haji Boghos Haji Sarkissian

Despite many appeals I continued to send the necessary assistance to my father, therefore my conscience is totally clear. I have also received letters of praise from friends with heads on their shoulders. One of them wrote:

August 1, 1911 Nirze[41]

To my generous brother Mr. Senekerim, of high character,

First of all, it is especially in order to ask about your gentle wellness. I hope you are healthy. If you ask your servant [the author means himself as a sign of humbleness], let me say that I read your letter dated July 4 and I am delighted with you[r news]. May God realize the wishes of your heart, my brother. After asking about everyone, you even consider children. When your letter arrived Kheder Agha was invited to Hamidian's wedding. He got Mihran married, I wish the same for you. I am sending my special greetings to my brother Garabed and asking his wellness with longing. I hope you are well and peaceful. I am also sending my greetings to Vahan and asking about his fragile health. Vahan, I have not heard a word from you since you left. Hereafter, you may or may not write, it's up to you. Give my greetings to all neighbors.

Eternal prayers,

Hagop S. Chelebjian

---

41. This letter too is in Turkish, using the Armenian alphabet.

Under the circumstances I was almost totally ignorant of community developments in my surroundings, until the advent of the European war [the First World War] and the Armenian *Aghed*.[42] Like many others I too started attending meetings and following the press. Finally, realizing that a person's highest calling is to help his country, I decided to become a member of one of the political parties. Of the four, I thought the Armenian Revolutionary Federation appeared to be the most popular. Therefore, I decided to dedicate myself to its flag. I became a member on December 20 1914. I remain a member to this day and will continue to be one until my death.

After my arrival in the United States my first place of residence was with a humble Armenian family. I had not yet in my life felt like a bantukhd. I had continuously lived at the paternal hearth, under the care of my father and mother. Because of the circumstances of life, I ended up in the bosom of *ghaributiun* [state of living in foreign lands] and I am fortunate that I encountered such a felicitous situation that saved me to this day from feeling like a bantukhd. As I said, at first I enjoyed the hospitality of an Armenian family that possessed the highest of qualities. There was in the family a white haired, God-fearing old woman with a smiling face, whom I called *mayrig* [mother] and she deserved the title in the true meaning of the word. She was from Arapgir but had spent most of her life in the Balkans. Her children had been educated in the Armenian community school system and were married in Bulgaria. Having had her daughter married to a half-educated man, they moved to America in 1906. The mayrig's name was Heghine Arzumanian. The other members of the family were Mihran and Mrs. R. Dodakian, and their children G. S. and Miss O. S. They were not rich, but they always lived a joyful and gay life. Mrs. R. was educated in Bulgaria and then in Bolis. During the three years I lived with them, I respected them as my own, and they respected me in return. They fretted over me as my mother had done. I cannot replace the favors that I enjoyed from that family and, for that reason, I have always had a feeling of gratitude toward them.

Mrs. R., as a reflection of her refined mind, often said, "If there is crudeness in Armenian family relations, if infighting and gossip are ever-

---

42. *Aghed* means catastrophe; it refers to what is now known as the Armenian Genocide.

present, if they lie and insult each other, if caring and empathy, humility and truthfulness are lacking, the Armenian child will inevitably be infected with that disease. We fathers and mothers see what high degree of responsibility we have in the upbringing of our future generation."

Her conversations were always about that and similar issues. "It is true," she would add on occasion, "that such disputes and discord happen occasionally under our roof too, but these things happen despite my position…"

I applaud with joy the much-appreciated step of such women and find laudable this progress of the feminine sex. Let the traditional chains be broken, chains that for centuries have oppressed our mothers and sisters. It will be the educated mothers who will lead the future generation, which is so needed by our emaciated and tortured fatherland.

My brothers

My eldest brother, Garabed, was born in 1883. After a few years of schooling, he was compelled to leave school because my father was alone and needed help at his work. In 1905, he was married to Miss N. Aselbegian. He had a good position in Nirze and was often involved in community affairs. After a while he roamed big Middle Eastern cities with our maternal uncle, such as Gesaria, Sebastia [Sivas], Ankara, etc. He did not contribute anything to the household during that period, but he did acquire some experience and self-education. He was extremely fond of companionship and loved the community too much. He organized feasts frequently during the winter months. He worked with my father for a short period and then opened a grocery store and had much success. Then one day we heard that he had left for America. For a few months he settled in Hudson and then he went to Watertown to work in the famous Hood factory. In 1910 I too came and joined him. After eight or nine months we decided that Vahan should come too, with Nuritsa [Garabed's wife]. Alas, our family harmony was disrupted after his wife arrived. For two years I gave my pay[check] to her without even opening the envelope. Vahan did the same. But my brother Vahan did not turn out what we expected him to be. Vahan became her first victim. I heard about it and kept silent. I was waiting for the end but my brother had left his reins in the hands of his wife.

One day I saw Vahan weeping. A thousand-and-one reasons crossed my mind. Perhaps our father had died, I thought, or something equivalent. Finally, after I insisted, he started telling the story.

"A few minutes ago, I heard laughter from the kitchen. I walked in and the moment they saw me they hid something and blushed. I saw that they held a paper used for letters from the homeland that they wanted to hide from me; I walked out without a word. The noises continued. A peculiar curiosity overtook me, I wanted to know what that was all about. Like a little devil I hid in a corner and listened. My God, I could have never imagined the kind of vulgarity my brother was hurling at our father. The noises I was hearing were not of laughter but of mocking mixed with his wife's 'hah hah' laughter. Apparently my brother tried, through his *bajanakh* [brother-in-law, specifically, wife's sister's husband] to have my father sign a loan paper for some imagined 100 gold liras my father is supposed to have borrowed. After answering with an absolute refusal, my father left for another village because of work. There he got into an argument with the müdir [chief] of the village, who slapped my father. And that was the reason for my brother's and his wife's joy."

Vahan stopped his story, but his tears continued running down his cheeks. I got up from my bed, extremely angry, but still not knowing what to say. How low evil can go, how hard crime can be! To have lived under my father's wing, jobless and sauntering, and then to demand a loan paper from him against a sum never given him. The fool was not thinking that he had many younger brothers who, nonetheless, were of higher intellect and had stronger arms, ready to sacrifice themselves for our father. I could not wait any longer. I entered the kitchen, and said very sharply, "You are no longer our brother. The undeserving son who relishes the slap received by that old man. Shame and curses. You must end your relations with us and with our father starting today."

To my angry words they tried to respond with an iron bar and a piece of wood. Naturally I needed to retreat and withdrew into [my] room and locked the door. I escaped a good beating through the intervention of some Marashtsis. That same day I left the house with Vahan. Peace returned to our lives and we dedicated ourselves to the task of helping our father.

There was a time when we needed money, but we preferred to borrow it.

Chapter 2

Garabed had three children: Vartuhi, Hovhannes, and Yeva, but I must say that we did not attend the birth or baptism of any of them. For three years we were not on speaking terms with each other. I should add that my former teacher, Mr. Hagop, played a nasty role in this disturbance by maliciously distorting the words of the sides. A while later we reconciled but that did not last long because of the unbearable behavior of his wife.

Vahan

My brother Vahan was born in 1894. He was a very tough adolescent with no desire to attend school. As a result, he earned the disdain of my father and my mother. We used to walk together and often we ended up fighting. He came to America in 1911. He too found refuge at Hood. After a year or two he followed the advice of others and quit that job in order to find a day job but eventually returned to Hood. On the outside he appears to be presumptuous and sly but he is very sincere and humble by personality. He has always been liked by people around him. His only fault is his lavishness. Until today he has not been able to save a cent. He is strongly patriotic and always sacrificing for his party. He has served time in jail with my mother when he was very young, scarcely nine months old. But where is he now? No need to say, he answered the call of duty, took his leave from us and showed by deed what he was preaching yesterday and the day before. His resting place is the field of honor...[43]

My paternal cousins

Currently I have two paternal cousins in America. Garabed Kh. Khederian and Garabed S. Khederian. The first, Garabed, was born in 1890. He was five or six years old when his father returned from Bolis. His father tried everything to teach his son all that he knew. But I think the teaching method he used made the child forget all of it. As a child Garabed was very smart, I remember learning the alphabet from him. He was still a school-aged youth when his father died. He had to provide for the living of his

---

43. As the author will inform later, his brother Vahan joined the Armenian Legion of the French Army as a volunteer to fight the Ottomans at the end of the First World War. The Armenian Legion was formed well after the Genocide was under way. Armenians in foreign lands who had lost their families joined that force, which was organized in Egypt, trained in Cyprus and fought in the eastern Mediterranean.

mother and five sisters. So, he left the school desk and book and went to a village called Belegesi to learn the craft of making cutlery. He worked for five years and was successful in providing for his family. His sisters' rug weaving helped a lot, of course. He came to America in 1912. In a short while, he paid his debt and started helping his mother. But the World War destroyed everything. He had no news from his sisters or his aging mother. But Garabed is still hopeful that the day will come when we will all return to our homeland, that we will reconstruct our destroyed homes, on the corpses of the biting vampires.

Garabed S. Khederian

Garabed S. is the son of my uncle Serovpe. Tall, well built, and very healthy. He was born in 1894. He was a weakling when he was young. His father was uneducated, and the son also did not attend school. For long years he worked very hard assisting his father in his shop. Of the two sisters and four brothers in that family he is the only one who survived. Recently, after his mother's death, he left their house unattended and came to America. Like the rest of us, he too was accepted in the community college, the famous Hood factory. With his savings of a few years, he became the owner of a shop in South Boston, where he remains to date.

Baruyr and Sarkis [my younger brothers]

Two unique names, sixteen and thirteen years old. The roses of the household, our only hopes for the future. Baruyr was endowed with good qualities. He was red cheeked, medium height, with blue eyes and blonde hair. His appearance corresponded to what was inside and he was always admired. He was devoid of any traditional shyness; he was the representative of a new generation. For him old or young, father and mother made no difference: he expressed himself like an adult, audacious and imperious. His level of consciousness placed him in the position of the "papa" of the Khederian clan. We knew him with pride and we doted on him with care. He loved education deeply and refused to miss school even for an hour. He studied languages and had made much progress. So many times, he wrote letters in English and demanded that I place him in an advanced educational institution: either Soorp Garabed or the college in Talas, that is where his mind was set. Here is a sample of his letters:

Chapter 2

November 7, 1913, Nirze
Honorable brothers Senekerim and Vahan,

I had the honor of receiving your letter a week before the current date. I cannot tell you, and my pen cannot describe the joy it caused me.

Ok, now, dear brothers, I have a request from you.

First, a six-shooter [a pistol, known in Turkish as alte atesh]; second, a watch; third a pair of rubber shoes; and fourth, a hat (cap). I want these things not just for my sake, but to uphold your honor too. Specially since you had already promised [to do so]. If you honor your word, then keep your promise.

Earlier I wanted to come to America. Now I have changed my mind. I will go to school here, to Soorp Garabed Monastery or Talas College, and get my diploma. On condition that you will send me my goods. I repeat that you must send me these items for sure so that I can go to school here.

Respectfully,
Your brother Baruyr Khederian

In 1913, after my father's death, I received some letters where my formerly education-starved brother said something different. He had demanded a pistol and a watch. This seemed strange to me. Yesterday's sheep was trying to act with me as a wolf. I wrote to others and was informed that without someone watching over him he had become cool toward the idea of schooling, and it led him to look at the outside world. Baruyr has always had deep love toward all of us. I have read all his letters with tears in my eyes, because all of them touch upon his premonition of death. Here are his lines:

December 2, 1913, Nirze[44]
My respectful and dear brother[s] Senekerim and Vahan,

Today is December 1. Sarkis Agha Avakian arrived on Sunday evening, but I could not visit him [yet] and get the news. You sent money for the problem of the vineyard. I am so happy. May God provide the wishes of your heart. Oh, my brothers, God does not countenance mother and father for me. Let's see what our end will be. What will I be? Will I

---

44. This letter is in Turkish, using the Armenian alphabet.

come there, or will you send me to a school? Let me know either way. If God gives health, all the things will pass away one day. Ah, Senekerim Agha [who knows] if we may see each other alive again. Are we devoid of even this [seeing each other]? I wish these black days had not come upon us, my dear brother. "I was born an orphan, I died poor, this world has not made me laugh."[45] I wish this sorrowful world had not made me like this. I have many things to write but my language falls short. I am not a poet as to write everything [poetically]. Don't judge me. Eternal well-being.

Your grateful brother,
Baruyr Khederian

I had taken the decision to bring him to stay with me. I sent a twenty gold lira check to Serovpe Effendi so that he would arrange for Baruyr to leave for America. Soon the crisis-filled European war arrived and Gesaria was involved in it. Soon I received a letter from Baruyr. He wrote that the day he was going to start his trip all carriages were taken over and there was a temporary order banning all travel. This is the first step of the future massacres by the kavtars [mean, evil persons]. I waited impatiently for a second letter. I received the letter, which contained more tragic news, that the government needs the assistance of the people and started its legalized loot. They took objects and foodstuffs. I sent another twenty gold liras through the Ottoman Bank. It has been three years and I have had no further news. I am sure my Baruyr was a victim of the criminals. I will plant my last kiss on your grave, dear brother, if it is ever possible to find your burial ground, I will ask in vain for the name of your killer. I have overcome your grief but what tortures me cruelly now is the fact that my revenge remains unrealized.

My little brother Sarkis was just an innocent child. Tall, with black hair, black eyes, always smiling and obedient. He would obey any order from his elders immediately. He had another fine quality. If anyone owed us anything, he would get the payment without even notifying us, indicating that he would be master of his own business once he grew up. But where is he now? Maybe he, along with thousands of other innocent children, expired under the Turkish sword.

---

45. A Turkish saying.

He never liked going to school. His only wish was to ride a horse or a donkey and for that reason he was scolded in so many ways. But he did not care. He wanted to occupy himself with household chores and our advice did not move him. In what state are you now, Sarkis? I know that you are either imprisoned in a cell or have fallen from a bloody blow. I am sure, though, that the blood of the innocent does not dry up until the flowers born from their blood is picked by close relatives, who will guess the crime committed by the vividness of the color of the flowers, crimes whose only witnesses are those flowers and the grass.[46]

My maternal uncle and his sons

Mikayel Haji Sarkissian was an old man and belonged to the bourgeoisie class. He never wanted to see anyone else advance, he always wanted to be the center of everything. The only way to accumulate wealth, as far as he was concerned, was to be stingy, and he never diverged from that principle. His wife, my grandmother, being diligent and obedient, helped her husband reach their goal. They had three boys and three girls: Haji Baba, Garabed, Haji Boghos, Yeva, Yeghisapet and Mariam. Haji Baba was stingy like his father and worked day and night. He married a girl form a well to do family. He had hardly reached his forty-fifth birthday when he died due to having worked excessively. His wife followed him within one month, leaving behind two children, Asdur and Mikayel. The latter's name was changed to Aghabey. Asdur was an active boy. Like his ancestors, he worked without complaining. He had taken upon himself all the concerns of the family and faced all its problems. I will briefly discuss Aghabey later.

Haji Boghos Haji Sarkissian

Since childhood, Haji Boghos has been extremely hardworking and rebellious; he also always disobeyed teachers and parents. From an early age he was taken by the love of revolution and abhorrence of the Turkish system. Soon after the Hnchagian party infiltrated the country, a branch was established in Nirze. Everyone became members, from the priest down to the last peasant. That did not last long due to persecution by the state.

---

46. Very little is known about the methods and sites of destruction of Armenians in Nirze Village. Some details can be found in Kenneth Cline's ""Flowers on a Grave," in Ararat Quarterly, Winter 1987.

Senekerim Khederian and Aghabey Haji Sarkissian (Boston, 1920s, photographer unknown, Nvart Chalikian papers, courtesy of Harry Parsekian).

Chapter 2

The chapter lost all its members and everyone shut their mouth except for my uncle. Haji Boghos had taken an oath, the oath of a real man, to remain forever faithful to his adopted idea.[47] And for years he fought against state persecution all alone. He would have been happy if the villagers had just remained indifferent and had not committed acts of betrayal and treachery. The poor man was even obligated to commit robberies in order to feed his family. He spent most of his life in prisons of big cities. Finally, he was pardoned and returned to the village, physically weak and his pockets empty.

Before being engaged fully in the revolution he had married my paternal cousin, who was a refined and delicate lady. Witnessing the tortures suffered by her husband, she ended up with heart disease. They had three daughters and one son: Yeghisapet, Sultan, Makreni and Hajibey. Yeghisapet was married at eighteen to a nice young man from Efkere, Avedis Akoghlanian. So many times, my maternal uncle's wife, Lusaper, was sent to prison carrying a child in her arms. As for the two other two young ladies, who knows which Turks' whims they were subjected to.

Hajibey was born in Nirze in 1893. He attended the village school for a short while. How could the poor child have the disposition to focus on his lessons when he witnessed the daily torture his father was subjected to? He worked as an ironsmith. He came to America in 1913 and, needless to say worked in "our" Hood factory. Although the son of a revolutionary, Haji Bey is not a fiery person. He is a modest and serious man, but also has liberal tendencies. He is trained in the use of arms as well. The national spirit is always present in him and he is always interested in the nation's affairs. He became a member of the Armenian Revolutionary Federation and I believe he will remain faithful until the end of his life.

Let us now talk about Agha Bey, whose life resembles a stormy sea. If I get into the details I would have to write a whole volume. He was born in 1888. His parents died when he was a year old, but because of the wealth they left behind, the child grew up under favorable circumstances. By the time he was seven years old he was already known as a mischievous boy. All

---

47. "Idea" is the literal translation of the Armenian word գաղափար, kaghapar. In 19th and early 20th century Armenian politics and literature, it also refers to an ideal, holy task, holy purpose.

the villagers complained about the damage he caused all around. He would cut down a fruit tree in order to have a cane. For someone who has always lived abroad, I do not find it superfluous to mention that he had not received any education. Growing up he used to go to the shop with his brother, not to work, but to assist in matters of trade. He was so clever and deceitful that many called him *jambaz* [acrobat]. He would insert himself in things he did not know about or did not understand. But the strange thing was that he always came out ahead. He was a first-rate horse rider and in the use of weapons, although that caused a number of misfortunes.

Wherever he was, at school, at a wedding, or elsewhere, his *bagh yergat* [literally cold iron; pistol, revolver] was always with him.

Whichever field he took his horse to graze, the owner would turn around and walk away instead of getting angry at him. Despite his debauchery, he had a princely vein in him, for which he was respected, especially by his friends and relatives. Social gatherings were not fun without him.

I did not get to see him before I left for America. A few months later I received a letter that informed me that Aghabey had married. I did not believe it and wanted to double check. And then H. Jelebjian informed me that soon after his wedding he was drafted into the army and that the many attempts to save him from military service had failed. For a rebellious boy like him army life would have been intolerable, especially under arbitrary Turkish military law. The Balkan War had already erupted and Edirne was at the center of the fighting. But due to his cleverness and vivaciousness, he was loved by everyone. He was not sent to the front, so he spent his time in comfort. When Edirne was occupied, his situation became uncertain. He planned on escaping and did so successfully. He spent a few weeks with my aunt in Bolis. And then, in 1913, he came to America. He too worked at Hoods, where he remains until now.

Hovhannes Kuyumjian

One of our close relatives in the village, by the name of Hovhannes Kuyumjian, started producing and using counterfeit currency with two or three friends, sometime around 1820. But the secret did not last long. The government found and hung the friends, but Kuyumjian himself escaped and got to Jerusalem. Soon after his arrival the king of Ethiopia came to

Chapter 2

Jerusalem for pilgrimage. Somehow Kuyumjian managed to make his acquaintance. It is said that at the time, Ethiopian currency was made of leather. Kuyumjian revealed his secret to the king and accompanied the king upon his return. Ten years later he became the Minister of Interior of the country. Although married in his homeland, he was compelled to have a second wife, for it was impossible to bring his wife to Ethiopia. Although living in a foreign country, he did not forget his homeland, and especially his first wife and children, [sending assistance] through Jerusalem.

One day his son Asdur, not satisfied with the assistance he was receiving, decided to go to his father. He went to Jerusalem and made inquiries with the vartabeds [celibate priests]. The vartabeds promised to pay him the sum he wanted without his going to Ethiopia. Convinced, the poor boy took the 100 gold liras and returned home. There are serious suspicions that the inhabitants of that stagnant den [the vartabeds] turned over to the family only a small portion of the huge sums that Kuyumjian sent them intended for his first family. Kuyumjian could not have sent the family directly because he was pursued by the government. Each time the vartabeds sent Asdur fifty or sixty gold liras, but the secret was revealed. But meanwhile H. Kuyumjian had died.

As I said, he had achieved a very high position and at the time of his death he bequeaths 400 million British pounds to his family in Nirze. That news reached the village through the newspaper *Azadamard*, and his grandson, Hovhannes Kuyumjian, got to work. Unfortunately, as the bequeather had not specified the name of the village, a number of Kuyumjians appear to have claimed the money, but not being able to provide proof, they failed. Our family spent a great deal of money to send someone to Bolis and pursue the affair. From Ethiopia Kuyumjian had gifted our village church one table cover and a chalice etched with the date and his name. That was the most important proof, so the will was certified by the Sultan and the Patriarch. The money was just about secured. One of Sultan Abdul Hamid's bodyguards, the Circassian .... Pasha, offered to buy the trial [pay off the claimant and own the rest] for 5,000 gold pounds. Unfortunately, the Constitution was promulgated, the Sultan was dethroned and Patriarch Ormanian removed from office. The Circassian Pasha escaped and the case was lost. Some think that the money was

Gesaria (Kayseri) with Mount Erjiesh in background, (postcard, Gomidas Institute archives).

appropriated by the Sultan and Ormanian, but we do not know to what degree that is the case.[48]

Asdur Kuyumjian

One of the offspring of the hopeless, imaginary wealth, [Asdur Kuyumjian] was born in 1895, the son of a well to do family. The family-owned big orchards in a village called Svghn. Hovhannes Agha had two boys and one girl, Garabed, Kiprianos, and Anna, none of whom received an education. Proud of their name, the boys invested in very big businesses, although they came out with losses. The only reason for that was their being illiterate. Kiprianos was married to my paternal aunt's daughter, Yeghisapet, and they had two boys and three girls. Asdur was the elder child, so the family responsibilities fell upon him. The poor boy learned

---

48. According to historian Boris Adjemian who has studied and written about Armenians in Ethiopia, Hovhannes Kouyoumjian was known as Haji Hovhannes, a jeweler in Adwa, a city in northern Ethiopia. Haji Hovhannes was apparently well known locally and by Western travelers in the 1830s and 1840s and had strong connections with the court. However, Adjemian states, many elements of the orally transmitted story about Hovhannes Kouyoumjian were exaggerations, including his having being a minister in the king's cabinet, having created the Ethiopian currency, or the sum bequeathed to his family having been so huge.

shoemaking but that was not enough to keep the family. Their maternal uncle, Yeghiazar, being a good-hearted man, helped the family as much as he could. One day Asdur got a letter from his father stating that it was essential that Asdur come to America. I sent him a ticket, and he arrived here in 1913. The first year he started helping his mother. Today, having paid his debts, he lives comfortably, anxiously waiting for the end of the calamity, hoping that he will find his mother and sisters again, even if in a half-dead state.

"News from Nirze"

On August 11, 1917, I received a letter from Khnus, signed by Melkon Müdürian. Müdürian wrote: There is hardly anyone left in Nirze, except for a few individuals. Turks from the surrounding villages took Nirze's beautiful girls. The letter writer also gave a number of names of persons destroyed by the hands of the beast. Any Nirzetsi who read the letter would be weeping. Mr. Melkon had participated in the Battle of the Dardanelles [April 1915], then went to Yerzinga and somehow escaped to Khnus. According to the letter, some Nirzetis are still alive in various cities, and a few young men are serving in the army.

Chapter 3

Nirzetis in America

Three or four Nirzetis came to America in the 1890s: Hovhannes Agha Torossian and his son Harutiune, and S. Avakian. They stayed in Lawrence [Massachusetts] for six or seven years, and returned to the homeland. This was during the time of the old regime and they were subjected to government pressures. As a result Nirzetsis didn't even dare utter the word America. The break lasted a long time. In 1909 the first traveler to America was my brother Garabed Khederian. He settled in Watertown [Massachusetts] and wrote very encouraging letters back home, so the whole youth of Nirze wanted to go to America. In 1910 I and two others came as well. The next year it was nine or ten who came. And even more the following year. Thus, from a village of some 130 households, in 1914 there were approximately seventy here, most having settled in Watertown.

In order to be helpful, I would like to give some information about Gesaratsis in this area. There are forty or fifty of them, mostly young. Looking at them at a glance one would feel proud of them. The sad thing is that very few of them are interested in national issues. There are no tradesmen or merchants among them, they are all factory workers. Alas, the domestic lives of a small fraction of them present sad pictures. There is a class of them, when examined closely or if you live with them, whose lives raise questions. Sad to say that some of them follow their lowly pleasures rather than living by noble and high ideals. Fortunately their number is small and it is decreasing with time. We wait with hope that all of them will soon be made pure.

As I mentioned, the majority of Nirzetsis lived in Watertown, so on April 23, 1913 they formed an Educational Union. The first banquet was held on April 20 1914, at 107 Arlington Street Cafe. All compatriots were present. A collection of funds produced $200. There arose a number of issues within the organization among the villagers, so that often there was a new executive installed at three-month intervals.

Often an executive committee was dethroned without having accomplished anything. Personal antagonisms played a very negative role in all of this. Until now the Union suffers because of some immature

Chapter 3

individuals. The second banquet of the Union was held on July 25, 1915. Since I have notes in my diary, I will reproduce them here word for word.

> The Project banquet of the Gesaria Nirze Village Educational Union occurred at Brighton's Reddy Hall, and present were all diligent compatriots. Chairman Aselbegian briefly explained the purpose of the gathering and then invited Mr. L. Baba Torossian and Mr. G. Vosgerchian, who explained the benefits of educational institutions. We had a wonderful time listening to the speakers of the day.
>
> The event became brighter with the short speech of Mr. H. Shaghoyan and his song in five langauges. The program came to an end with the solo songs of Messrs. Sarajian, Torossian and G. Nazarian. The second part of the evening was the free eating and drinking. It seemed that forgetting the horrible news from the homeland, the guests enjoyed group songs and toasts in the warm atmosphere and camarederie. The collection produced $228.10.
>
> In addition to the financial benefit, the banquet was also of great moral uplift. But the excessive use of liquor and the passing out of some of the men brought a sad end to the evening.

On September 26, 1915, the Union held a general membership meeting in the ARF Club. An examination of our finances showed that the Union had $600.77 cash on hand. The same day we decided to organize a program event or a play to assist in the cause of Armenian liberation. However, enchanted by the beneficences and pleasures offered by this country, we, the local Gesaratsis, have not forgotten mother Armenia and we will not forget our fathers [and] our mothers, who are dying for lack of a morsel of bread. In view of this *zulumnahar* [tyranny-stricken] state of the Armenian nation, and on the basis of the decision of the membership, the executive of the Union proceded to present a play in Union Hall. The play was presented on May 30, 1916, with the help of the ARF "Dzovag" actors troupe. Some 1,000 tickets were printed, and due to the active work of our compatriots a lot of tickets were sold. The problem is that many of our compatriots have not yet paid for their tickets, the committee has been lax in its work, and the accounting remains up in the air as of today, May 10, 1917.

Soon after the play the money was supposed to have been sent to the Catholicos. So many needy Armenians are hungry, thirsty, naked, and barefoot, while we here spend time in our soft beds and we don't make any effort to hasten our assistance.

Nirtzetsis undertook another action, and had much success in that instance. Since I have the description of that too in my diary, I present it here.

> A few young men from the Nirze village of Gesaria, having in mind the cause of Armenian liberation, decided to convene a meeting for fundraising purposes, in order to have performed our duty and to add our cents to the thousands collected already. Immediately all compatriots are informed and invited to attend the meeting in Mr. G. Karageozian's room at 89 Elm Street. Some thirty compatriots had gathered there at the designated time. Following some discussions, the speaker of the day, Mr. G. Karageozian took the floor. After presenting the purpose of the gathering, he invited those present to express their views. At that period there was a bitter struggle between the ARF and the Union for National Defense. Driven by the same dirty antagonism, a few of those present presented some unproven arguments but were not successful. It was decided that we should proceed with the fundraising. These few demanded that the collected funds be sent to the Catholicos or to the Union of National Defense here in the US and left without giving a cent.[49] We started our work and collected $300. We elected a committee that would appeal to those who were not present and were hoping that the new committee would be successful. But unfortunately that new committee too

---

49. The dissension described here is representative of the conflict within Diasporan communities for decades. In one form or another that conflict pitted two segments of the communities: The ARF or Tashnag party and its affiliated organizations versus the Hnchagian and Ramgavar parties and other organizations opposed to ARF. In this case The National Buro was the body controlled by the ARF raising funds for resistance and volunteer fighting forces, while the relief drive sponsored by the Catholicos of All Armenians in Etchmiadzin (near Yerevan) and the Union of National Defense was supported by anti-ARF forces. Compatriotic societies often had members from both sides, which caused rifts or worse within these associations.

Chapter 3

ended up with disagreement. After the meeting was dispersed, a few from those who had left the meeting approached the committee, threw insults at the ARF and the National Bureau, and convinced a few of its members to divert the money to the Union of National Defense. And that started the cultivation of the darnel grass.[50] Prodded by these individuals, a few of the committee members did not agree to send the money to the National Bureau through the "Hairenik." This dirty dispute continued for a few weeks. Realizing that the end would not be good, it was decided to invite a second meeting to achieve some kind of agreement. The second meeting convened on February 7, 1915, with the participation of sixty-five compatriots. After long discussions once more we failed to reach agreement. The decision was then taken to do the least of the two evils. Each participant was given two pieces of paper, one with the name of the Catholicos, the other marked National Bureau. Each participant was free to decide where his contribution should go. The meeting ended with an ugly situation. The amount designated to the Bureau was $250; the Union of National Defense ended up with $100. Those of us believing in the National Bureau sent the money through the Central Committee of the ARF with the following message:

Enclosed you will find a check for $250 to be sent to the National Bureau, the funds having been collected by some dutiful villagers of Nirze, Gesaria, with the purpose that is common to all Armenians, support of Armenian freedom, which is possible to obtain with the fighting force produced by the ARF. The young men believe in the ARF as the party of action in the Armenian reality. Like a steely shield, it faces our centuries-old enemy. With countless heroes, it enjoys the hope and faith of Armenians in general.

Long live the Armenian Revolutionary Federation

Long live Armenian liberation

Long live the Armenian volunteers.

---

50. A reference to darnel grass that looks like wheat, but is not actually wheat; the expression refers to the act of exposing people who are not what they say they are.

The lifestyle of Nirzetsis of America and our "union"

As I have mentioned, my brother was the first to come to America from Nirze. He rented a room in Watertown and lived a most comfortable life. More Nirzetsis came in time, and almost all followed his example until they set aside enough money. Today all Nirzetsis without exception have a regular life. They occupy a leading place in Watertown, so they live in the most stylish of rooms no matter what the rent.

Just as the others who came to America, we too rented a house (one floor) and lived there, but not as a "single," since we had furnished it normally. There were six or seven of us, who lived harmoniously because we were all from the same clan. These are names of the members of the group: The author of these lines; my paternal cousins, S. Khederian and G. Kh. Khederian; my brother Vahan; my sister's son, Asdur; my maternal cousins, Aghabey and Hajibey; and my sister's husband, G. Müdürian. These seven individuals lived with so much love for each other, as if they constituted one soul and one body. This union was formed in 1912. The members of the union were all individuals of clean character. All suggestions were accepted unanimously. That was the politics of mutual rejection. They all said yes, yes or no, no, and this is the way all issues were settled, even the most complex ones. The house was furnished neatly; we had as much furniture as any family would. For that reason sometimes we tried to prepare our meals at home. After a few months we would get bored and we would decide, unanimously to go to a restaurant, and we would do so. We lived such an enviable life for three or four years. We organized a feast every Sunday, and we had enormous joy and pleasure. The joker amongst us was Aghabey. He always made us laugh. We thus reached the winter of 1917 when we decided to prepare our meals at home. We had had enough of the restaurants. This decision was taken in our residence at 81 Arlington Street. We continued that way for three or four months. With as much harmony as was possible. We think that this was as comfortable as we had ever been since we came to America. We had tasty meals thanks to my brother-in-law Mr. Garabed Müdürian. We had wine brought directly from California, two casks. We thought this was the first winter we had enjoyed.

The happy and joyous days passed and then came the sad and black ones, with gossip, infighting, lies, and insults against one another. As if the heartbreaking news coming from the homeland were not enough, for we were reading about the death of our dear ones of hunger and thirst in the newspapers. These ugly things made us forget, it seems, all the past days. The reason for all of this change was one person only, who came like the devil into our holy family and upended everything. He lied, gossiped, accused, invented and maligned. He forced the holy union to be destroyed. All were honorable individuals. There was then a decision to separate before problems became bigger. We parted with teary eyes. No one [even] cared about claiming his belongings. He had passed the measure of calumny and limit. The five-year-old union was shattered because of one person, who is ..... He also had a partner in his evil work.[51]

General list of Nirzetis by city

In Watertown

Number		Age
1.	Senekerim Khederian	27
2.	Garabed Khederian	34
3.	Garabed Kh. Khederian	28
4.	Vahan Khederian	24
5.	Garabed Margossian	45
6.	Soghomon Margossian	30
7.	Yeprem Aselbegian	43
8.	Krikor Seferian	36
9.	Sarkis Seferian	27
10.	Arsen Seferian	24
11.	Armenag Seferian	24
12.	Garabed Seferian	24
13.	Serovp Seferian	21
14.	Hagopig Seferian	25
15.	Stepan Hajnlian	35
16.	Khacher Torossian	27
17.	Hagop Torossian	23
18.	Garabed Torossian	52

---

51. The person the author is referring to and the accomplice remain unknown, as do "the ugly things" in question.

19.	Toros Torossian	20
20.	Stepan Mekhjian	26
21.	Haygazun Tavitian	22
22.	Kerovpe Manigian	25
23.	Onnig Paglayan	44
24.	Haygarmen Nshanian	25
25.	Garabed Cheyrekjian	25
26.	Armenag Emjiyan	28
27.	Mgrdich Emjiyan	24
28.	Garabed Emjiyan	55
29.	Garabed Sarajian	25
30.	Garabed Zakarian	28
31.	Hapet Kehyayan	23
32.	Garabed Kehyayan	44
33.	Missak Kehyayan	26
34.	Sarkis Parseghian	33
35.	Missak Parseghian	35
36.	Garabed Parseghian	20
37.	Garabed S. Müdürian	34
38.	Garabed H. Müdürian	33
39.	Missak Hagopian	36
40.	Hagop Minassian	23
41.	Harutiun Minassian	30
42.	Asdur Kuyumjian	21
43.	Aghabey Haji Sarkissian	29
44.	Haji bey Haji Sarkissian	24
45.	Khachadur Haji Sarkissian	22
46.	Mihran Karakochian	25
47.	Armenag Haji Khacherian	27
48.	Rupen Haji Khacherian	31
49.	Garabed. N. Parseghian	37
50.	Krikor Abajian	31
51.	Stepan Keriyan	42
52.	Yeghiazar Abajian	25
53.	Taniel Margossian	46

Chapter 3

54.	Krikor Margossian	23
55.	Khachig Haji Bedrossian	26

In Boston

56.	Yeghiazar Hovsepian	31
57.	Harutiun Torossian	34
58.	Nerses Torossian	31
59.	Stepan Balian	24

In South Boston

60.	Garabed Khederian	24
61.	Avedis Mudirian	27
62.	Kasbar Mudirian	31
63.	Garabed Aselbegian	38
64.	Setrak Kehyayan	34
65.	Sarkis Tekerian	35
66.	Krikor Baghdatlian	38
67.	Kalusd Tekirian	35

In Detroit

68.	Hayg Haji Bedrossian	26
69.	Hampartzum Hagopian	33
70.	Garabed Kehyayan	32
71.	Garabed Budakian	50
72.	Harutiun Budakian	23
73.	Arsidages Baghdatlian	26
74.	Hovhannes Torossian	28

In Newton Upper Falls [Massachusetts]]

75.	Mihran Hajenlian	34

In Roxbury [Massachusetts]

76.	Haji Nshanian	48
77.	Garabed Ghalayjian	33
78.	Setrag Ghalayjian	26

In Akron [Ohio]

79.	Hovsep Aselbegian	37
80.	Missak Aselbegian	28
81.	Yeghia Aselbegian	25
82.	Jibrayil Aselbegian	22
83.	Srabion Kalzakjian	27
84.	Dikran Sareyan	31
85.	Mihran Nshanian	22

In New York

86.	Harutiune Pavlian	34
87.	Armen Pavlian	26
88.	Garabed Hajenlian	32
89.	Hagopig Parseghian	30
90.	Stepan Alyanakian	22

In Washington, D.C.

91.	Sarkis Nshanian	43
92.	Mihran Seferian	28
93.	Yeghiazar Balian	27

In Malden [Massachusetts]

94.	Armenag Karakochian	28

In Hudson [Massachusetts]

95.	Garabed Karageozian	8
96.	Missak Karageozian	34

In Racine [Wisconsin]

97.	Mgrdich Haji Sarkissian	32
98.	Haji Sarkis Haji Sarkissian	26

In Queens [New York]

99.	Dadur Margossian	34
100.	Harutiun Aselbegian	29

Chapter 3

Those who returned to the homeland

Serovpe Manigian	33
Sarkis Kehyayan	31
Sarkis Avakian	55
Krikor Kehyayan	35
Onnig Mekhjian	43
Parsegh Seferian	45

Volunteers [in the Armenian Legion and the Caucasus]

Khachig Haji Bedrossian (Caucasus)
Vahan Khederian
Mgrdich Yemjian
Garabed Aselbegian
Hagop Torossian
Yeghiazar Abajian
Stepan Balian
Stepan Alyanakian (Caucasus)
Garabed Sarajian (Caucasus)

The deceased

Hayg Abajian	24
Krikor Balian	20
Stepan Alyanakian	22
[Hapet Kehyayan ?]	

Those who returned to the Homeland

A few of those on that list, having worked here for two or three years and thinking their future secured, returned to their native hearth. These were Serovpe Manigian, Sarkis Kehyayan, Sarkis Avakian, Krikor Kehyayan, Onnig Mekhjian and Parsegh Seferian. They were all married individuals with children who, naturally, could not have stayed [long] under foreign skies. They all returned with joy and happiness; they had missed their fatherland. They missed their dear children. They missed their dear wives. Finally, they missed the air and water of their homeland. But alas, the tyrannical Turkish claws caught them before even the dust had been cleaned from their traveling shoes. Under the guise of a military draft, the Turkish government moved them to unknown destinations in groups. Mountains and vales, stones and grass will have become witnesses as to what happened to these tall and sturdy young men who returned. They left America in a hurry to find their dear ones, but it turned out that they returned to be burned alive on the soil of their homeland. Our fathers, mothers, sisters were raped by Muslim mobs, imprisoned in harems. It was one thing that the latter were already in the country and their fate was unavoidable. But what can one say about those who went from America?

We hear mythical things about them. Sometimes, it was said, since they had come from America, they must have money, and the government used the excuse of the *bedel* [cash payment to secure exemption from military service] to extort money from them. Sometimes we heard that they were shot in the threshing floor of Soorp Krikor [Monastery] because, having come from America, they were considered more dangerous. Whatever was the case, the truth is that they suffered the same fate reserved to our whole nation.

Oh, you honorable young men, why did you leave free America? Was it to have your blood mixed with that of your dear ones? Did you go in order for our dead to remain without graves? I am sure that your blood dyed rivers. You fell on the sides of mountains alone, were left defenseless in fields, your corpses became feed to ravenous birds, your cries shook the heavens. We have all become aware of all this, we know it all. The day of reckoning will eventually come, you will rise from your graves and shout, "Strike at the Turkish mob so that they see what it means to annihilate young men like us." We have not forgotten you. For the love of fatherland and to take revenge for your deaths, we crossed a thousand miles over the ocean and reached the front lines of the Caucasus, and we fought on the mountainsides of Vasburagan. We killed and were killed, and continued the fight for reckoning until today. Thousands of young men answered the call from the Caucasus. And today too we hear a new invitation to fight, and within a few weeks thousands of young men enlisted to go as volunteers and shed their blood.

This time we will come to you... We will come to our historic homeland to see you and to take the revenge you have bequeathed us. Do not think that the glory and joys of America have restrained us or have turned off our patriotic feelings. No, we will come to you ... and we will see your unburied bodies. Perhaps that will constitute consolation for us.

We will bow at your bloodied corpses and tell you that we have come to take your revenge.

Respect for your memories, dear compatriots.

The life of Nirzetsis in America

Four or five Nirzetsis returned home before the outbreak of the European War. A few others were getting ready to do the same but fortunately they changed their minds. One of those was A. Karagochian. He had quit his job in the factory and was all ready to return to his beloved homeland. But by chance his bank book disappeared, some bad guys lifted it from his satchel while he was not watching it, and he was compelled to stay a few more days. That delay became the reason for his not returning home, since Turkey entered the war during those days and no Armenian would return home for fear of being conscripted in the army. Thus, Armenag was spared certain death.

After Turkey entered the war some Nirzetsis, such as M. Karagochian, A. Karagochian, G. Torossian and the author of these lines, received telegrams asking for money and all of us paid up, without exception. The telegrams came from Gesaria through the Ottoman Bank. The sad thing is that as of today we have not received any responses. In addition to losing our fathers, mothers and sisters, we also lost our money. There were between fifty and sixty Nirzetsis in Watertown, and every week we received twenty to thirty letters from the homeland. There have been no letters since the start of the war, except for a few that caused us more grief. One of those letters came to my maternal uncle, Asdur. This is what the letter said:

"My dear brothers, Since I was an ironsmith I was left behind, and I am now named Ahmed. Don't wonder about us. The wolf ate the sheep. There is no one left in the village, we don't know where they went. That appears to have been our fate."

Still, Nirzetsis expected to receive letters from the places where their families were driven. But we did not even have that kind of luck. Nirzetsis could not control themselves at what was happening and we undertook a project. We collected sufficient funds. We telegraphed the American Ambassador in Turkey to try and gather for us as much news of Nirze as possible. This task was supposed to have been performed by Mr. Svazlian. It has now been approximately one year. We have not received any news, and Mr. Svazlian has not returned our money.

Nirzetsis have quite a bit of interest in national affairs. They attend meetings, participate in good faith in fundraising by community institutions. Almost all Nirzetsis are optimistic regarding the national question. The pessimists are few. The number of party members is also low; about five to ten are members of the ARF and Hnchagian parties, and a large number sympathize with one or the other. In addition to participating in national affairs, Nirzetsis also provide financial and moral help to individuals in need. One of those individuals was Father Mesrob of Efkere. Having found himself in a dire condition, he came to Watertown. Nirzetsis came together immediately, and with each contributing two or three dollars, the sum of $100 was secured.

The life of Nirzetsis in America has a negative dimension in that they are factory workers. The surprising thing is that Gesaratsis are supposed to be good merchants, most should have become businessmen, while today the businessmen among them can be counted on one hand. Without exception, Nirzetsis are well dressed "chic" young men. They spend all that is required to be fed and dressed well. *ers, Since I was an ironsmith I was left behi*For that reason, they are all healthy, vigorous, vivacious young men. Those from other provinces treated Nirzetsis with respect. But all Nirzetsis have a bad habit. They use Turkish, although they all know Armenian. This is to be condemned. Still, all of them know how to read and write, and almost all are familiar with the Armenian language. They don't speak Armenian because often they are derided by those who are Armenian speakers. As if that damned Turkish language had penetrated our meat and bone.

Gesaratsis in America have almost all become owners of good businesses. In New York the biggest rug dealers are Gesaratsis. And in Boston the factory workers all have good positions and receive satisfactory wages.

Armenag Pavlian

Armenag Pavlian was born in 1891 in the Nirze village of Gesaria into a middle-income family. His father, an ironsmith, died in 1910. His mother was Yeghisapet. He had a brother by the name of Harutiune Pavlian. He had two sisters, one of whom died two years after getting married.

Armenag focused on his education. He never wasted a minute. He wanted to help his family even at the age of ten or eleven. That is why he labored at home in whatever time he had available. One day, during the year end examination [at the school], Mr. Vahan Kurkjian, one of his relatives, a maternal cousin, attended the session. Mr. Kurkjian, Director General of Gesaria schools, saw that Armenag had a bright future and remarked that Armenag should continue his education at a higher level. Armenag's brother took it upon himself to pay every expense, and Armenag was sent to the American high school in Talas.

On September 5, 1902, he left Nirze for the Talas high school and remained there for seven years. He won many prizes during those seven years and he always came first in his class. A few months after graduating with highest honors, he received an invitation from the Armenian school of Evereg to teach English. He taught in that school for one year and then returned to his birthplace, Nirze, and started teaching there, although he had agreed to teach in Soorp Asdvadzadzin school of Gesaria at a higher salary. But he preferred to teach in his birthplace. He strengthened the teaching of English in the school and also instituted a course for teaching French.

Like others, Armenag also left for America, on August 28, 1912 and reached New York on November 17, 1912 to be with his brother who was a tailor. Armenag's aim in coming to America was to go to school for a few years and then obtain a medical diploma. But despite his wishes, he was unable to realize his plans and was compelled to become a factory worker. Currently he works in one of the hospitals of New York, and has an important and easy job. Armenag is moderately nation loving. Having made significant contributions in the homeland, he is now an active member of the ARF New York Committee.

Nirzetsis who died in America

Nirzetsis who came between 1909 and 1918 incurred a few regrettable deaths.

Hayg Abajian

The first was Hayg Abajian, who after four years of painful years in a hospital, died on May 10, 1916. Hayg was born in Nirze village and had hardly reached his twenty-fifth year. Details about his life and burial can be found in the *Hairenik* daily.

Krikor Balian

Born into a poor family, Krikor Balian was modest and spoke little. It seemed he had inherited his father's poverty; he had no luck with his American plan, either. On his way to America when he was in Patras, his money was stolen, and the poor boy was left without any money. He was forced to return to Bolis without any money. His older brother in America, S. Balian, provided new funds for him to once more sail for America. He got to America, but on account of his age and height he was unable to find a suitable job. He began to work as a dishwasher in restaurants. But how could a small boy endure such a difficult life? Naturally, he would become ill. Within a few months the youth's face started turning yellow, with hardly a trace of blood. The doctors who examined him diagnosed him with tuberculosis and recommended that he return home. The poor brother spent more money to send him back to Gesaria, believing that the water of the homeland would help. But, hardly reaching Bolis, [Krikor] ended up in Soorp Prgich Hospital and within ten days, he died at the age of eighteen. This is the life of the factory worker. "There is no life on earth for the factory worker, because he has not achieved consciousness."

Stepan Alyanakian

One day we received a telegram announcing that Stepan Alyanakian had drowned. This sad news circulated amongst all of us and there was no one who had known him who did not mourn this young man's death.

He was born in Nirze village in 1893; like others, he came to America to make a living. Unger[52] Stepan was modest and quiet, but by personality he was unswerving. He had a deep sense of the responsibility he was bearing as an Armenian. Recently he had joined the ranks of the ARF. When the volunteer movement started, Unger Stepan could not control

---

52. The word means "friend," but also comrade. Armenian political parties used it to refer to other members of the party, in the sense of "comrade."

Chapter 3

himself.[53] He left his comfort and chose to walk the path of blood. On August 24, 1915, he left for the Caucasus and participated in all the battles. Because of certain circumstances he returned to America as if lost, and went back to his job. But still, he was restless and wanted to join the fighting. When the second volunteer movement[54] started again he could not stand aside. He enrolled as a volunteer, to leave through the National Union of New York... But he could not achieve his dream. While swimming on the New York beachfront he drowned due to a confusion. May you rest in peace, Unger.

(For details, see the September 1, 1917 issue of the *Hairenik* daily.)

Hapet Kehyayan

The Nirzetsis had three or four deaths in America already when, as if that was not enough, we buried another young man, Hapet Kehiayan, in this foreign land. He was born around 1892, into a middle-class family. He came to America almost four years ago, but did not find success in any job he pursued. Recently he had the misfortune of having a sore on his arm and was unable to work. His uncle, Garabed Kehyayan, had recently bought a farm and invited Hapet to stay with him, hoping the healthy air of the farm would help his nephew. But poor Hapet passed away in his youth. Hapet had not received an education, but he loved his nation and joined the H[nchagian] Party at least to make his financial contribution to national projects. May he rest in peace.

Nirzetsi volunteers

We have received letters from all the Nirzetsi volunteers I had mentioned earlier in this volume. They have all reached safely in their training camp. An unfortunate accident struck the ship taking them from Marseille to

---

53. The reference is to the first Armenian volunteer fighting force organized in 1915 during the First World War as an adjunct of the Russian army then fighting against the Ottoman Empire.
54. The second volunteer fighting force was organized on the Russian side of the Caucasian front during the war. Its purpose was to assist Russian forces reach Armenian villages and towns in the Ottoman Empire before they too were massacred by the Ottoman forces.

Port-Saïd. The ship sank, but all had the good luck to be saved and were not harmed. They are all in Cyprus.

I received a letter from my brother Vahan. He informed me that "the training is over and now I am in Egypt and will be headed to the battlefield in a few days." He writes, "If there are skeptics in America, send them over here, let them see the Armenian army. I am sure that the most alienated will become the most nation loving."[55]

Diar [Sir][56] Vahan Kurkjian

I will not attempt to present here a biography of Diar Vahan Kurkjian but will offer only a brief sketch for the readers of this book.

Vahan Effendi Kurkjian was born into a very poor family. His father, Sarkis, was a carpenter by trade; he could hardly secure his family's subsistence. His mother, Sima, was a very clever woman from the Khederian clan and helped her husband in a way by making clay pottery. By a stroke of luck Vahan was sent to Soorp Garabed Monastery. I should say that Vahan had been the most advanced student in all of Nirze. Vahan studied in the monastery for seven years and graduated first in his class. He was immediately invited to teach in Gesaria, and in a few years he became the best paid teacher. The Ordutsis, having noted Vahan's capable performance and his abilities, invited him to teach in their city and promised to pay him a higher wage. But Vahan Effendi returned to Gesaria after hardly a year had passed due to the unfavorable weather conditions.

This time he was called into a higher position, as Director General of their school system.

---

55. Vahan Khederian, the author's brother, returned to America, resettled in Watertown, Mass., and remained active in community life. He was a dedicated member of the Armenian Democratic Liberal Party. As a volunteer in the Armenian Legion he became a highly respected leader who committed acts of heroism that were not forgotten by his comrades-in-arms. He was remembered fondly by a few of them in the Boston based newspaper, *Baikar* daily, the organ of the party, where his brave deeds are detailed. Vahan Khederian died in October 1976. His obituary, along with a lengthy story narrating his life, appeared in the same month in *Baikar*.

56. The word Diar, տիար, is an Armenian honorific used instead of Mr. for highly respected and honored gentlemen.

Chapter 3

Nirzetsi Legionnaires or volunteers (from the original Armenian edition, date, place and photographer unknown).

Before Mr. Vahan's arrival in Gesaria, the city had no middle school. They were all neighborhood schools, with primary school programs. Mr. Vahan aimed at establishing a secondary school and he succeeded. He succeeded because the people of Gesaria had great trust in his management capabilities; they knew the value of each recommendation he made. I should add that Mr. Vahan earned such basic respect and trust as a man of irreproachable morals, because of his honest personality, and especially for his steady, strong, and hard work.

Mr. Vahan was able to unite the few primary schools of Gesaria, which became the Soorp Sarkis middle school and he became the school's director and teacher until his martyrdom.

Mr. Vahan had many merits, which could be presented in the following manner:

1. He was extremely modest, to the point that if judged from the exterior he would be viewed as a very shy person.
2. He knew the value of his words and speech, and had a sober demeanor to the point that all his students adored him. During his

many years of teaching there was not a student who was hurt by him, on the contrary, all of them respected him from near and far, they were interested in him, often cooperating with him in his public activities.

Diar Vahan Kurkjian performed ably the position entrusted him.

After the declaration of the Constitution, he became very active in public life. He started a collotype publication, *Shepor* [bugle], while he used to fight against conservative forces; and, with the help of the ARF, he succeeded in removing Bishop Drtad Balian as the prelate of Gesaria.[57] For a period of time, he was also the active editor of the *Hayrig* weekly.

He was a man of few words, but inside the classroom he was impressive and likable. He had the undeniable talent to teach, and we must say that before and above all he was the teacher-principal. He knew how to get along with his colleagues and his position as principal made him more liked rather than provoke passions and personality conflicts.

He was a convinced liberal. He was a member of the local ARF Committee, and was always active in party activities. He, along with another beloved *Tashnagtsagan* activist in Gesaria, Mr. Kevork Vishabian, with whom he was closely associated, had his authoritative voice in a wide circle of sympathizers regarding each of the major events in Armenian public life.

In one word, Mr. Vahan Kurkjian was one of the central figures of Gesaria.

As the father of a family, he was an irreproachable and affectionate man, steadfast in his principles and convictions, and a first-rate administrator.

The whole region knew him, and he was always invited to participate in activities in Gesaria Armenian organizations. He was often a member of

---

57. Bishop Balian was a conservative clergyman, otherwise highly respected, who seems to have been despised by Armenian revolutionary groups. He appears to have preferred to work closely with Ottoman officials as the best way to keep Armenians safe. After the 1908 Young Turk Revolution with whom Armenian revolutionaries were cooperating, he was caught between old and new authorities and forced to resign.

Chapter 3

governing bodies of educational and political organizations. He was a trustee of Soorp Garabed Monastery.

He had a major role and voice in the placement of teachers in the Gesaria region. Many took up positions in this or that institution on the basis of his recommendations. He paid special attention to the educational progress of the villages and worked toward placing virtuous teachers there.

Vahan S. Kurkjian was one of the best known and most prominent figures in Gesaria and surrounding areas. He was loved by the Armenian public, appreciated by official bodies, and respected even by those who were his antagonists in public life. He was an educational leader with many years of service.

Doctor Khachig Doevletian and Vahan Effendi Kurkjian became victims of Turkish barbarism. Mr. Vahan had one final opportunity to escape death, but he returned to Gesaria not wanting to desert his educational work, his family, and party circles.

They spoke their last words with their smiling faces and pleasant expressions from the gallows: "We will die on the gallows but many will come after us and will herald the rise of the impending dawn."

Us Gesaratsis will remember with pride the names of these two national and party activists and those of many others. His [Mr. Vahan's] memory must remain unforgettable in the hearts of his co-villagers. His and Vishabian's testimonies from the gallows must remain always in the minds of Nirzetsis. They are our precious victims and their revenge must move us each minute.

Respect to the selfless martyr.

The letter that follows can offer an idea of how admired Mr. Vahan was by his students and by Gesaratsis. Being a close relative of Mr. Vahan, this letter was written to this author.

Honorable Sir Senekerim Khederian
Watertown
Dear Compatriot,

It may be strange for you to receive a letter from an unknown writer. Although the identity and name of the author of this letter are unknown to you, he would be familiar to you as a Gesaratsi. The common pain, the specter of our despicable fate, brings together not only compatriots but also co-nationals living miles apart.

Travelers on a sinking ship wish, instinctively and unconsciously, that most of the survivors be their own acquaintances. Like that ship, in this global conflagration those of us, the damned in general, and Gesaratsis in particular, with nests looted and destroyed, brothers slaughtered, we wish to receive some definite information.

The second flock of the cranes coming from America visited the brave people of Suedia.[58] Among those visitors I found one of the close relatives of our beloved Diar Vahan Kurkjian and your brother, Mr. Vahan Khederian. It seems that the school memories sleeping under the dust of four years stirred and I remembered our dear teacher Vahan Effendi Kurkjian incessantly.

Gracious, the paragon of honesty, with his smile that flourished on his head while being hanged—a monument to freedom—as if to herald the joyous morning of the rising sun.

The remembrance of happy memories during difficult days caused a storm in my heart as in that of your brother, because the bitter cup of pain and suffering was being offered to all of us equally.

Your brother informed me that I have a brother in America and [asked] that we occasionally correspond. I gave my agreement immediately. Dear compatriot, I do not wish to give you more trouble with this first letter by making this letter longer than it need be.

I remain your pain-sharing compatriot,

Manuel G. Beylerian

October 9, 1917, Port Said

P. S. You will want to know, of course, who is the author of this letter.

I, the undersigned, a native of Gesaria, was born in 1894. I received my primary education in Gesaria, in the United National School. The late Diar Vahan Kurkjian was the most capable principal of that school for four years. He became the victim of the cunning Turkish (Ittihad)

---

58. Musa Dagh is a cluster of Armenian villages in southern Armenian Cilicia, currently southern Turkey. Musa Dagh became famous for its 40-day resistance to Ottoman forces in 1915, as a result of which they were able to be saved by a French ship.

government. In 1913, when I graduated from that school, I came to Cairo on the advice of Diar Vahan. After three years of working as a secretary in various places, it has now been five months that I am in Port Saïd, in the camp of the refugees from Suedia as a teacher of national history and geography. But I lack the resources both for history and geography. I do not have a textbook of history or a world map. You understand the rest.

Same

Volunteers to the Caucasus front

The following Nirzetsi participated in the first volunteer movement: Garabed Sarajian (currently in America); Khachig Haji Bedrosian (according to some he is in Persia); Sdepan Alyanakian (recently drowned in New York). These volunteers participated in battles as permitted by the conditions.

On the path to duty

Defenders of the Armenian Cause

To escape the Turk's conscription
We came to America leaving behind father and mother
Hardly seven years have passed with untold pain
Alas our young lives became insignificant

Damned by the day we were born
Once born we should not have grown up
Our feet should have been broken so we could not come here
Our eyes should have gone blind so we would not have seen

Our ears should have gone deaf so we would not have heard
Rise up oh brothers, rise up quickly
We never achieved our dreams,
Fate has struck us

Onward, always onward, ... down with the chains of slavery.

Legionnaire Vahan Khederian, the author's brother (191?, Port Said, Egypt?, property of Rose Mamishian, Vahan Khederian's daughter, photographer unknown, courtesy of Harry Parsekian)]

Chapter 3

When in 1917 the news spread by word-of-mouth that volunteers were needed, the following Nirzetsis responded and enlisted: Vahan Khederian, Garabed Aslbekian, Mgrdich Emjian, Yeghiazar Abajian, Hagop Torossian and Stepan Balian. The Nirze Educational Association thought it proper to organize a banquet to honor the above volunteers. The banquet was held on May 30, 1917, in Boston. (For details on that event see the June 22, 1917 issue of the *Hairenik* daily.)

These compatriots had a very comfortable life in America. But they left that peaceful life to answer the call of duty. They left for a road that was snakelike, that was bloody, but they accepted all obstacles because they felt the nation's persecutions and miseries, they knew the tortures, thrashings, and rapes to which the nation was being subjected. This unprecedented *zulum* [tyranny, oppression] was taking place from Persia to Armenia to Cilicia.

These duty-bound and selfless Nirzetsis knew that Armenian honor was violated, that Armenian children were passed through the sword, that they were sold as slaves for a *mejidiye* [silver coin] or less. They knew that their brothers were destroyed under the guise of military conscription. The selfless Nirzetis knew that rich or poor, the Armenian was deprived of his property and had not even the opportunity to remember it in exile. Thousands of women and children, old and young, fell on the road of their escape, because they suffered from hunger on the one side, and exhaustion on the other. The young, duty-bound Nirzetsi men knew that delicate Armenian women and girls were being chased by Turkish *zabtieh*s [gendarmes], sword and fire behind them, mountain and vale ahead of them, in snow and storm, without knowing where they were headed.

It is these facts that made these young men rise up and compelled them to assume their responsibilities. This is the picture of our adored fatherland. Although in America for a long time, they were not enamored by the mores and pleasures offered by this land, they had not forgotten Mother Armenia. These young men followed national life and read Armenian stories. Because they followed the example of those heroes who rejected the chains of slavery and the vile chain of repression. Of course, that is the education that twenty or thirty years of revolution had taught. We are reaping the fruit of that history today. Anyone who studied the history of that revolution will see that the brave and patriotic gave themselves and the last drop of their blood for the freedom of their fatherland, for the glory and well-being of their nation. These were the events that fired up these young Nirzetsis, and drove them to the thorny road ahead... go take revenge on the lowly enemy.

It is you and similarly patriotic young men who will bring about the ideal of which we have dreamed for 500 years. "Go there, the Cilician world is calling you." Our compatriots are going where there are graves, death, torture, and dying. There they will see brave and patriotic ones who have fallen midway on the road by cruel hands and crushed under blows, burned on mountains and in ravines. I am sure that they will approach the martyrs resting under their cold tombs, they will feel their warm breath and noble ideals. They will listen to their graves, and will know that even their bones shout for life and rebellion. Oh, you Nirzetsi young men, God forbid should any of you be martyred, we will erect monuments to your name and we will place wreaths at monuments to your memory. You Nirzetsi knightly spirits, should you be martyred, the fatherland will be saved, and should you become martyrs, the fatherland will be resurrected.

Oh, you are to be envied because you will be the first to see the freedom of the Armenian world. You went voluntarily to perform your duties. If you happen to be martyred, your graves will become our chapels and your memories will be our pride. Oh, you Nirzetsi young men, go with arms in your hands, and you will tell the dog Turks, did you enter the war in order to slaughter the unarmed and defenseless Armenian women and children? Tell the Turks that this is the beginning of your end, you man-eating monsters. Will we leave so much blood and crime unpunished?

Therefore, dear and unforgettable compatriots, move forward, toward action, toward arms, and toward development. Move forward from the bloody road toward your duties. Come out as men to show the spirit of your action, show your talents, your skills, that is how our hopes will be realized. You, selfless Nirzetis, you are the ones who will welcome the morning of freedom that will flower from today's bloody ruins. You are the ones who will make the Armenian flag wave from the tops of the highest mountains of Armenia. Therefore, long live liberated Armenia, long live liberated Cilicia, and long live the Armenian volunteers.

P. S. Before this writing was sent to the printer, I learned that my maternal cousin, Haji Bey Haji Sarkissian, and his brother-in-law, Avedis

Chapter 3

Akoghlanian, left on September 22, 1917 for the above-mentioned purpose. I wish success to their patriotic sentiments.

Last Minute

The following two Nirzetsis have been called upon to serve in the American army: K. Manigian, M. Kehyayan.

The [Armenian] Population of Nirze Village and Their Wealth (Before the 1914 War)[59]

Population	Number in Family	Wealth in Gold liras[60]
Krikor Abajian	3	250
Hayg Abajian	2	200
Avedis Akoghlanian	4	300
Garabed Alyanakian	4	600
Assadur Aselbegian	5	200
Assadur Aselbegian	12	4,000
Asua Aselbegian	5	4,500
Garabed Aselbegian	4	200
Haji Hagop Aselbegian	4	4,000
Harutiune Aselbegian	4	450
Yeprem Aselbegian	4	100
Sarkis Avakian	6	600
Garabed Avedikian	3	300
Hovagim Avedikian	4	300
M. Khachadur Avedikian	3	500
Nerses Avedikian	5	900

59. The list appears to be incomplete, since it is missing many native families, including some mentioned in this volume. In addition, the listing in the original Armenian appeared to be random. The editor thought an alphabetically arranged listing offered many advantages.

60. The author does not provide a definition for wealth or a source for these numbers. A family would own a home, could own vineyards and orchards, a business and cash on hand. By all indications most of the Armenian families in the village could be considered middle class.

Name		
Onnig Babayan	3	200
Krikor Babayan	4	250
Arisdages Baghdatlian	4	150
Krikor Baghdatlian	3	100
Garabed Bardzamian	6	200
Garabed Budakian	3	200
Garabed Barsamian	3	500
Haji Balian	3	150
Harutiune Balian	6	500
Onnig Balian	3	100
Yeghiazar Balian	7	700
Bedros (Prod)	2	150
Hagop Beojukian	4	225
Khachadur Cheyrekjian	5	150
Hovhannes Cheyrekjian	6	600
Khacher Cholakian	8	300
Manug Cholakian	9	300
Sultan Domjigian	3	400
Garabed Ejeyan	4	225
Yeghia Emjiyan	8	500
Yeghiazar Gedrian	7	1,000
Hampartzum Ghalayjian	8	650
Antreas Goshgarian	4	300
Garabed Goshgarian	3	100
Yeghia Goshgarian	6	150
Garabed Guluyan	5	325
Harutiune Guluyan	4	800
Hovhannes Guluyan	6	175
Avedik Haji Bedrossian	12	900
Avedis Haji Bedrossian	4	700
Garabed Haji Bedrossian	4	200
Hagop Haji Bedrossian	4	600
Har. Haji Bedrossian	3	200
Hovh. Haji Bedrossian	5	500
Kevork Haji Bedrossian	4	200
Bedros Haji Khacherian	7	2,500
Krikor Haji Khacherian	9	1,500
Haji Haji Khacherian	6	600
Hovhannes Haji Khacherian	6	400

Chapter 3

Markar Haji Khacherian	4	900
Asdur Haji Sarkissian	6	3,000
H. Haji Boghos Haji Sarkissian	6	3,500
Kapriel Haji Sarkissian	7	500
Srpuhi Haji Sarkissian	7	750
Mgrdich Haji Sarkissian	5	425
H. Sarkis Haji Sarkissian	4	500
Sarkis Haji Sarkissian	5	275
Kerope Hajnlian	5	200
Sdepan Hajnlian	5	250
Mihran Hajnlian	3	200
Yeghiazar Hovsepian	3	500
Avedis Jelebjian	6	1,500
Hagopjan Jelebjian	2	900
Levon Jelebjian	3	400
Kerope Kalpakjian	5	1,000
Serope Kalpakjian	6	900
Setrag Kalpakjian	5	300
Srabion Kalpakjian	3	800
Giragos Karageozian	6	2,555
Mardiros Karageozian	2	1,500
M. Avedis Karakochian	7	5,500
Azadade Karakochian	7	3,500
Garabed Karakochian	4	150
Garabed Karakochian	12	5,525
M. Kapriel Karakochian	4	5,000
Krikor Karakochian	6	4,100
Vartan Karakochian	5	600
Bedros Kehyayan	6	225
Garabed Kehyayan	6	425
Khachadur Kehyayan	6	300
Krikor Kehyayan	4	200
Nshan Kehyayan	5	200
Sarkis Kehyayan	4	150
Sarkis Kehyayan	4	250
Setrag Kehyayan	4	200
Pilibos Keoshgerian	8	250
Sdepan Keriyan	6	400
Sdepan Khederian	4	200

Serope Khederian	4	500
Khacher Khederian	5	400
Kheder Khederian	8	700
Srpuhi Khederian	2	300
Hovhannes Kuyumjian	9	450
Garabed Kuyumjian	6	400
Hovhannes Kuyumjian	[blank]	250
Garabed Manigian	5	550
Harutiune Manigian	7	600
Garabed Margossian	7	500
Garabed Margossian	4	300
Hagop Margossian	2	175
Kevork Margossian	6	75
Tan[i?]el Margossian	6	525
Sdepan Matossian	5	550
Onnig Mekhjian	5	500
Nazar Minassian	5	100
Baghdassar Müdürian	4	400
Garabed Müdürian	2	400
Garabed S. Müdürian	6	600
Harutiune Müdürian	9	5,000
Kerope S. Müdürian	9	2,500
Melkon S. Müdürian	3	200
Mgrdich Müdürian	5	1,500
Simon Müdürian	4	300
Kasbar Nshanian	8	1,500
Onnig Paglaian	6	300
Mgrdich Parseghian	6	425
Nazar Parseghian	4	250
Nshan Parseghian	5	400
Parsegh Parseghian	5	200
Garabed Pavlian	5	275
Sarkis Pavlian	2	250
Hagop Sareyan	4	225
Jivan Sareyan	4	300
Dikran Seferian	9	500
Jivan Seferian	4	400
Khacher Seferian	4	200
Parsegh Seferian	7	600

Chapter 3

Sarkis Seferian	8	800
Sefer Seferian	8	800
Haji Yeghia Solakian	7	7,000
Garabed Tavitian	6	700
Bedros Tekirian	5	50
Kalusd Tekirian	3	50
Sarkis Tekirian	4	200
Garabed Torossian	6	400
Hagop Torossian	5	300
Harutiune Torossian	5	425
Hovhannes Torossian	9	900
Khacher Torossian	5	400
Garabed Yessayan	5	475
Serope Yessayan	7	350
Stepan Zabnian	2	150
Simon Zabnian	7	150
Garabed Zakarian	4	350
Hagop Zumbulian	5	700

TOTALS
FAMILIES   150
PERSONS   762
WEALTH   125,500[61]

---

61. The totals calculated by the author for his own list require small adjustments. Here are the correct numbers: Total number of families: 151; total number of persons, 775; total wealth: 107,715 gold liras. Also, for some unknown reason, the following 11 family names do not appear on this list: Ghazarian, Jeknavorian, Kiferzian, Kurkjian, Manukian, Markarian, Mgrdichian, Saroyan, Shakarian, Srabian, Tashjian, Yegiazarian. There could be others too.

There have been other numbers offered for the totals for Armenian families and persons living in Nirze at the start of the First World War. The difference in number is often due to the different ways families are counted. Whatever the differences, the number before of Armenians individuals for that period in Nirze is between 800 and 850.

GOMIDAS INSTITUTE
42 BLYTHE RD
LONDON W14 0HA
ENGLAND

www.ingramcontent.com/pod-product-compliance
Lightning Source LLC
Chambersburg PA
CBHW071626170426
43195CB00038B/2140